PARIS

in Stride

First published in the United States of America in 2018
by Rizzoli International Publications, Inc.
300 Park Avenue South
New York, NY 10010
www.rizzoliusa.com

Designer: Claudia Wu
Rizzoli Editor: Martynka Wawrzyniak

2018 2019 2020 2021 / 10 9 8 7 6 5 4 3 2 1

Distributed in the U.S. trade by Random House, New York
Printed in China
ISBN: 978-0-8478-6125-5
Library of Congress Control Number: 2017962716

PARIS
in Stride
AN INSIDER'S WALKING GUIDE

Jessie Kanelos Weiner & Sarah Moroz

New York · Paris · London · Milan

BATIGNOLLES-
MONCEAU

17e

9e

ÉLYSÉE
8e

LOUV

1e

16e
PASSY

PALAIS-
BOURBON 7e

6e

LUXEMBOU

15e
VAUGIRARD

14e
OBSERVATOIRE

BUTTE-
MONTMARTRE
18ᵉ

19ᵉ

ENTREPÔT

PÉRA

10ᵉ

BUTTES-
CHAUMONT

BOURSE
2ᵉ

TEMPLE
3ᵉ

POPINCOURT
11ᵉ

20ᵉ
MÉNILMONTANT

HÔTEL
DE VILLE
4ᵉ

ᵉ

NTHÉON

12ᵉ
REUILLY

MÉTRO

13ᵉ
GOBELINS

Contents

Introduction

Paris is a ceaselessly mythologized city. Many wistfully extoll the beauty, the history, the architecture, and the gastronomy of the French capital; it is only natural that visitors come with the ambitious aim of extracting the very best of its sights and its tastes. The concrete ways to go about this, however, can be daunting.

Travel guides tend to reference iconic venues and neighborhoods that reiterate what people have already gleaned about Paris from afar—it's easy to romanticize, especially since the city's reputation precedes it. This, however, is not a generalist's guide to the City of Light; rather, it is a handbook intended for those curious to explore the metropolis beyond the obvious routes. We want to showcase the ins and outs of Paris from a local point of view. We're two expats who have each spent a decade living in, and continually revisiting, the city's offerings. Consider us your local Paris friends who know the lay of the land: We know just where to get perfectly crisp bread, sip a robust cup of coffee, and take in the greatest selection of art. We purposefully want to highlight a vision of Paris that is not reductive: neither the tousled *"je ne sais quoi"* mystique of the *Parisien/ne,* nor the stodgy reverence for centuries of French tradition. We know these viewpoints are commonly exported and overly trafficked; luckily, they are not the only lenses through which to view French culture.

Paris in Stride is intended to be helpful both in terms of cultural decoding and in terms of ease in circulation. Even in unfamiliar territory, we want visitors to feel that they can make their way seamlessly in various neighborhoods. We address the odd snail-shaped arrondissement structure in an accessible manner: Suggestions are clustered according to the way one would naturally encounter them on foot, rather than according to the—somewhat arbitrary!—numerical chronology of the arrondissements.

Each section has a map of the neighborhood, equipped with an ideal walking route and a map key, and short descriptions of carefully selected spots to enjoy or observe. We also provide some destinations with no routes but with an assemblage of must-sees. Lastly, we have five dedicated sections with insights about how to tackle the essentials of Paris: the abundant delicacies, the elegant buildings, and the market stands.

Overall, we encourage an adventurous approach: Visitors can follow our walks, or use them as jumping-off points to explore whatever catches their eye. The compilation of historical sites, gardens, restaurants, cafés, galleries, boutiques—each with evocative illustrations—collectively provide an authentic glimpse into Parisian life. We're so pleased to share it with you.

—Sarah & Jessie

Latin Quarter & Île de la Cité

4TH & 5TH ARRONDISSEMENTS

Starting point:
GARE D'AUSTERLITZ

The city alongside the Seine has two strata: street-level bustle and a more serene route on the cobbled quai, which provides a respite from the urban frenzy. Nearby, eddies of tourism peak around major monuments. The islands of the Île Saint-Louis and Île de la Cité, once playgrounds of the aristocracy, are today quiet and calm residential capsules that draw visitors with their beauty and history. Notre-Dame de Paris ("Our Lady of Paris"), the medieval cathedral on the Île de la Cité, is widely considered to be one of the finest examples of French Gothic architecture and is among the most well-known churches in the world. On the south side of the Seine, known as the Left Bank, the Latin Quarter is home to a number of higher-education establishments (such as the École Normale Supérieure, Panthéon-Assas University, and the Jussieu campus). An epicenter of student life, the neighborhood is so-called because the Latin language was once widely the language of learning. Further east is a marvelous hub of flora and fauna, the Jardin des Plantes, with its zoo and museum, connecting the city to a sense of nature and repose.

❶ GARE D'AUSTERLITZ

Built in 1840, this train station takes its name from the Battle of Austerlitz, one of the most decisive tactical victories of the Napoleonic Wars. Classified as a historic monument—with its canopied roof and

gabled exits—the station was used as an *atelier de fabrication* for gas balloons in 1870. **85 Quai d'Austerlitz 75013**

② JARDIN DES PLANTES

This elegant garden was spearheaded in 1635 by Louis XIII as a dedicated space for the study of medicinal plants; trees planted by naturalists during the 17th century still flourish. Today there are 12 smaller gardens within the *jardin,* including those specializing in alpine plants, vegetables, and peonies. There are 45 staff gardeners who tend to the 15,000 plants and 8,500 varietals from a myriad of natural contexts, ranging from European smoke trees to curry plants, Persian silk trees to hybrid 'Star Wars' magnolias, handkerchief trees

to *Edgeworthia chrysantha*. It is a magical spot that showcases a vivid palette. **Quai Saint-Bernard 75005**

② MÉNAGERIE

Opened in 1794, the Ménagerie of the Jardin des Plantes is one of the oldest zoos in the world. The buildings, classified as historical monuments, reflect this patrimonial architecture—from the Palais des Reptiles (built in 1870) to the Grande Volière (the aviary, built in 1888) to the Art Deco Singerie (monkey house, built in 1936). The Ménagerie encompasses some 1,200 animals, including mammals, birds, amphibians, insects, and crustaceans. Up to a third of the zoo's species are under threat of extinction (including red pandas, snow panthers, orangutans, and turtles of the Seychelles). **57 Rue Cuvier 75005**

❷ᵇ LABYRINTHE

At the epicenter of this small labyrinth in the Jardin des Plantes stands one of the oldest metallic constructions in the world: the Gloriette de Buffon. This kiosk was built in 1788 in honor of the Comte de Buffon, a French naturalist and cosmologist instrumental in transforming the garden into a major research center. (Fun fact: His brain was allegedly placed within the base of a statue in the natural history museum; see #2d). Though the structure seems rather modest, the choice of material—high-quality forged iron—was innovative for its time, preceding Gustave Eiffel's use by a century.
40 Rue Geoffroy-Saint-Hilaire, 75005

2c GRANDES SERRES

Greenhouses were originally designed to conserve and acclimate rare botanicals that naturalists brought back from far-flung explorations: the oldest Parisian example was built by Sébastien Vaillant in 1714 to maintain a coffee plant gifted to Louis XIV. At the beginning of the 19th century, metal-and-glass structures were deemed the best insulators to mimic original environments. Charles Rohault de Fleury, the architect of the nearby Muséum National d'Histoire Naturelle (see #2d), built what would become prototypes of modern greenhouses, which were steam-heated. Today, the greenhouses in the Jardin des Plantes house everything from tropical rainforest ecosystems to desert-style plants from the Sahara to scrublands and mangroves from New Caledonia. **57 Rue Cuvier 75005**

2d MUSÉUM NATIONAL D'HISTOIRE NATURELLE

Architect Jules André completed this wondrous and immense hall, articulated in metal and wood, in 1889. Tiered, balconied floors—which, overall, hold some 7,000 natural history specimens—are over-hung by a glass canopy. *The Grande Galerie de l'Évolution* is a sight to behold, filled with diverse species. The *séquence-de-résistance:* an elephant-led parade of African savanna taxidermy including lions, hyenas, zebras, giraffes, buffalos, cheetahs. The holdings of the museum range from South American tropical forest jaguars to Ant-arctic harp seals. It's a destination that's fun for kids and adults alike. *36 Rue Geoffroy-Saint-Hilaire 75005*

❸ GRANDE MOSQUÉE DE PARIS

The French parliament voted the Grande Mosquée into being in 1922, as an acknowledgement of Franco-Muslim efforts in World War I. Completed in 1926, it was built in the *mudéjar* style, that is to say it featured medieval Iberian architecture and decorative Moorish workmanship. Inspired by the Alhambra in Grenada, the mosque features a 100-plus-foot (33-m)-high minaret. The venue draws visitors of all creeds to its prettily tiled patio sprinkled with outdoor seating, where one can enjoy small glasses of mint tea plucked from circulating trays. (Handle gingerly; the tea is always piping hot!) There is also a restaurant, Arabic language library, and hammam, or Turkish bath (bring a bathing suit if you plan to use it). ***2 bis Place du Puits de l'Ermite 75005***

❹ INSTITUT DU MONDE ARABE

A secular counterpoint to the Grande Mosquée, this venue fosters cultural dialogue between the Middle East and Europe. In 1981, President François Mitterrand secured its Seine-side location. Jean Nouvel won the design competition for the project with a concept of embedded photosensitive *mashrabiyas*—a type of lattice-worked window—across the entire facade. The building was inaugurated in 1987 and won the Aga Khan Award in 1989. Be sure to take in a view of the city from the top floor. ***1 Rue des Fossés St.-Bernard 75005***

⑤ LA RÔTISSERIE D'ARGENT

This former *bouchon lyonnais*—a signature type of restaurant in Lyon that serves copious and meat-heavy cuisine (think sausage)—was acquired in 1989 by Claude Terrail, who shifted the joint's orientation to a prototypical *bistrot parisien*. Its ever-turning aromatic *rôtissoire* is central to the hearty spirit of the eatery. It is not just a neighbor to the Tour d'Argent (a Michelin-starred historic restaurant), but the two venues in fact share quality producers and a philosophy of seasonal cuisine. ***19 Quai de la Tournelle 75005***

⑥ PONT DE SULLY

The Pont de Sully, which links the 4th and 5th arrondissements across the Seine, was constructed in 1877 under Haussmann's renovation of Paris. It is named after Maximilien de Béthune, the 16th-century duke of Sully. The bridge's design, set at a 45-degree angle to the riverbank, enables a splendid view over the quais of the Île Saint-Louis and Notre-Dame, as does its neighbor, the Pont de la Tournelle. ***Pont de Sully 75005***

❼ ÎLE SAINT-LOUIS

The Île Saint-Louis is one of two natural islands in the Seine. It is connected to the rest of Paris, and to the neighboring Île de la Cité, by bridges. One of France's first examples of urban planning, it was mapped and built end-to-end during the 17th century. Aristocrats, wealthy businessmen, and politicians in the 17th and 18th centuries came here to live away from the inner-city noise. Today, most of the island is residential, but there are small businesses and one stately church. The island is named after Louis IX (Saint Louis), the French king from 1226 to 1270. Entertainers (musicians, jugglers, mimes) often perform on a small bridge that connects Île Saint-Louis with Île de la Cité—the epitome of charm or cliché depending on your point of view! *Île Saint-Louis 75004*

⑦a ÉGLISE SAINT-LOUIS-EN-L'ÎLE

Constructed in 17th century, the Église Saint-Louis-en-l'Île was designed by François Le Vau (brother of the ambitious architect Louis Le Vau, who contributed to the designs of Château Vaux-le-Vicomte and the south wing of the Palais du Louvre). The charming village-like edifice—a clock hangs from the bell tower—is the only church on the island. The ornate baroque-style interior contrasts sharply with the rather austere facade. *3 Rue Poulletier 75004*

⑦b BERTHILLON

Berthillon is a family-run artisanal ice cream business: In 1954, Raymond Berthillon got the *turbine à glace* while working in the hotel/café he bought and tested his recipes on the Île Saint-Louis's local schoolkids. Berthillon uses only quality ingredients in its ice creams: whole milk, crème fraîche, fresh eggs, vanilla beans, and cacao butter. The sorbets feature fruits like cassis, citron, and mango plus flavors like pear caramel, mandarin chocolate, and apricot raspberry. These toothsome treats draw in the crowds. Each day, Berthillon makes about 1,055 quarts

(1,000 liters) of ice cream and sorbet for both the boutique and the 140 Parisian restaurants, brasseries, chocolatiers, and épiceries it supplies. *29-31 Rue Saint-Louis-en-l'Île 75004*

❽ SQUARE JEAN XXIII

Located behind—heck, practically glued to—the Notre-Dame cathedral, the Jean XXIII square is only a tiny remove from the swarm of tourists, but it is a welcome enough distance. The apse of the cathedral is a stunner, made all the more picturesque by Japanese cherry trees, hazelnut trees, and the ivy that lines the stone walls bordering the Seine. **4 Parvis Notre-Dame—Place Jean-Paul II 75004**

❾ SHAKESPEARE AND COMPANY

This English-language bookshop has been a Left Bank darling—and veritable pilgrimage point—for writers and readers since 1951. The bookshop was founded by American George Whitman in a 17th-century building that was originally a monastery, and drew literary types like Allen Ginsberg, William S. Burroughs, Anaïs Nin, Henry Miller, and James Baldwin. The open-door policy to "tumble-weeds"—writers, artists, and intellectuals invited to sleep among the shop's shelves and piles of books—has brought streams of young creatives on-site, including once-unknowns like Darren Aronofsky, Geoffrey Rush, and David Rakoff. In 2006, Whitman's daughter Sylvia took over the management of the shop; she introduced a novella-writing contest open to unpublished writers, a Shakespeare and Company publishing arm, and an ambitious number of literary events per week (with such compelling guests as Zadie Smith, Lydia Davis, Edward St. Aubyn, and Jeanette Winterson). The adjoining café has great treats and a picturesque view of Notre-Dame. *37 Rue de la Bûcherie 75005*

⑩ FONTAINE SAINT-MICHEL

This monument, located in the Place Saint-Michel, was designed by the architect and trained neoclassical sculptor Gabriel Davioud during the French Second Empire. There are two winged dragons on either side of the fountain, the figure of Saint Michael and the devil, and statues representing the cardinal virtues. Unlike prototypical Paris fountains, it integrated color, notably Corinthian columns of red marble from the Languedoc region. Today, it is heavily trafficked by tourists, and you run the risk of getting kicked in the head by a break-dancer. **Place Saint-Michel 75005**

⑪ GALERIE KAMEL MENNOUR

This gallery, housed in a renovated 17th-century *hôtel particulier*, represents contemporary international artists like Daniel Buren, Lee Ufan, and Camille Henrot. The gallery regularly collaborates with institutions for off-site projects, such as the Monumenta exhibitions at the Grand Palais and the French Pavilion presentations at the Venice Biennale. In 2013, a second exhibition space debuted around the corner. If you walk between the two, you'll notice a plaque at 7 Rue des Grands-Augustins alerting pedestrians to Pablo Picasso's former atelier, where he painted the infamous tableau *Guernica*. **47 Rue Saint-André des Arts 75006 and 6 Rue du Pont de Lodi 75006**

⑫ BOOT CAFÉ

The original Boot Café across the river was so-named for the pocket-sized cobbler business it took over. Its newer cousin is much more spacious—with rustic wooden beams, a glassed-in kitchen, an array of plants and greenery, a floor-to-ceiling display of international travel books—but with similar design cues, notably yellow and green plastic stools, marble-topped bistro tables, and white tiling behind the bar. The kitchen turns out light salads and hearty bowls of congee porridge, while also serving its signature craft coffee and cakes. **26 Rue des Grands-Augustins 75006**

⑬ MARIAGE FRÈRES

During the 17th century, brothers Nicolas and Pierre Mariage began voyaging on behalf of the royal French court: Pierre went to Madagascar for the French East India Company, while Nicolas made several trips to Persia and India. Successive generations remained in the tea trade and, in 1854, founded the Mariage Frères Tea Company. In today's shop, the elegant warmth of the wooden displays are filled with oversized tea tins. At browsing level, there are samples to inhale in all varietals: green, black, smoked, rooibos. Selections are carefully weighed on old-fashioned scales and packaged in branded black sachets. The company has multiple tearoom locations in Paris, and is also served in first-class grand hotels such as Le Meurice. *13 Rue des Grands-Augustins 75006*

⑭ MONNAIE DE PARIS

France's longest-standing institution, the Monnaie de Paris, was officially founded in 864 (!) as a coining workshop in Paris attached to the crown. In continuous operation since its opening, the mint is also, as of 2014, a space for contemporary artist installations, inaugurated with American artist Paul McCarthy's exhibition *Chocolate Factory*. With rotating temporary exhibitions, the space hosts projects by international contemporary artists tailored for the lavish salons and *escalier d'honneur*, creating an interesting dialogue within this UNESCO-recognized patrimonial edifice. **11 Quai de Conti 75006**

HOW TO NAVIGATE A
Market

Open-air markets are an incredibly vibrant part of French living. They're colorful, sensuous, loud, bustling, and inspiring to both home cooks and great chefs. The heaps of products are a bright palette cleanser relative to Paris's beige tones; the available tastes and scents are plentiful with possibilities for to-go picnics and sit-down meals. They're a ritual and a pleasure.

Each market operates two days a week (with the exception of Marché Aligre, which occurs six days a week); there are multiple options per arrondissement. Market hours run from early morning to early afternoon.

5 TOP MARKET TIPS:

1. Circulate before buying. Many stands will have similar offerings, but survey before committing so as to get a sense of both price and quality.

2. Seek out the farmers. Look for a sign that proudly says *producteur/ maraîcher*. Many sellers buy from the Marché de Rungis, the wholesale market outside of Paris not far from Orly airport. Farm stands will have a smaller selection that is more strictly seasonal and based on the yield of the local land, including things you won't find elsewhere. These sellers will indeed be more expensive, but provide better quality.

3. Take a good look at the price. It's often marked on a tiny chalkboard and hung from the stand—but sometimes items are sold individually, in a grouping, or per kilo. Keep small change on hand to speed up purchases. At the end of the market, usually around 2 p.m., sellers may cut you a deal to get rid of their excess.

4. Look for the long line. People come to the market regularly (often weekly), and build a chatty relationship with their sellers (from "how's your son doing?" to "what's the best way to prepare these potatoes?"). That fidelity, and a willingness to wait, is usually worth betting on: it's an investment in good service and a nod to quality that locals have carefully cultivated.

5. Don't be afraid to reach for an available sample—or even to request a taste of something if no sample is provided. But don't automatically serve yourself, even if you want to buy. Some sellers are extremely particular about being the ones to bag their items, so check before you get into a snippy exchange with a vendor.

5 MARKETS TO TRY

MARCHÉ BASTILLE (Thurs & Sun) one of the most sprawling; Blvd Richard Lenoir 75011; M° Richard Lenoir

MARCHÉ RASPAIL (Sun) all-organic products; Blvd Raspail 75006; M° Notre-Dame des Champs

MARCHÉ ANVERS (Fri 3pm-8:30pm) night market; Square d'Anvers & Ave de Trudaine 75009; M° Anvers

MARCHÉ PRÉSIDENT WILSON (Wed & Sat) most cultural location; Ave du Président Wilson 75016; M° Iéna

MARCHÉ ALIGRE (Tues-Sun) open six days a week; Rue d'Aligre and Place d'Aligre 75012; M° Ledru-Rollin

Le Marais 3RD & 4TH ARRONDISSEMENTS

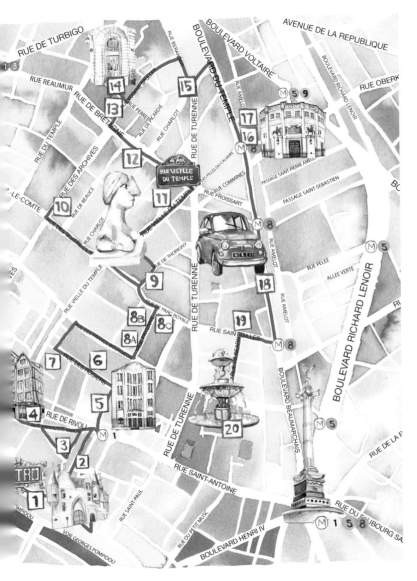

Starting point: MÉTRO PONT MARIE

Le Marais is one of Paris's oldest neighborhoods, dating back to the 13th century. Indelibly marked by its history, it spans Henri IV's manicured Place des Vosges as well as lesser-known treasures like the Art Nouveau synagogue facade by architect Hector Guimard on Rue Pavée. The area was once peopled by aristocrats and noblemen and their extremely opulent residences, until the French Revolution disrupted that reality. This lavishness is still very much evident in the urban landscape, where hôtels particuliers—translation: private mansions—abound, many of which have been turned into museums and administrative buildings (in order to maintain the cost of their preservation and upkeep). The area contains not only historical sites, however: it is also replete with discreet green spaces, gay bars, the city's archives, traditional Jewish locales, a dedicated Picasso museum—all close-knit neighbors. Le Marais may no longer be aristocratic, but it is certainly fashionable in a contemporary way, its past legacy offset by modern "musts": trendy cafés, young galleries, and clusters of hip boutiques.

① BIBLIOTHÈQUE FORNEY
& JARDIN DE L'HÔTEL DE SENS

Completed in 1507, the Hôtel de Sens is a Middle Ages–Renaissance blend of architecture with gothic flourishes and distinctive corbelled turrets. In the late 1800s, it served as a kind of learning annex for local artisans, and before that, it was the headquarters of an archduke, a queen, a laundry business, and a jam maker (not all at once, though that would have been something!). To date, it houses the Bibliothèque Forney, a fine-art and architecture library and museum, its function since the early 1960s. The manicured garden behind the building features perfectly contoured geometric hedges, convincingly evocative of 17th-century-style landscaping, though the garden is in fact only a few decades old. *1 Rue du Figuier and 7 Rue des Nonnains d'Hyères 75004*

❷ RUE DU PRÉVÔT

To get to Rue Saint-Antoine, snake down the ultra-narrow Rue du Prévôt, its width shrinking from around 10 feet to 6 feet (3–1.8 m). Once named Rue Percée (you can still spot the old sign), the street likely does not differ too extensively from what it must have looked like at the beginning of the 18th century, with many of its original structures preserved. *Rue du Prévôt 75004*

❸ MAISON EUROPÉENNE DE LA PHOTOGRAPHIE

Opened in 1996 in the former Hôtel de Cantobre, restored and reconstructed by architect Yves Lion, the Maison Européenne de la Photographie (MEP) presents regular rotations of temporary exhibitions, featuring iconic contemporary photographers like Joel Meyerowitz, Sebastião Salgado, David Lynch, Harry Gruyaert, Bettina Rheims, Andres Serrano, Bruce Davidson, and Bernard Plossu. *5–7 Rue de Fourcy 75004*

4 MAISON À L'ENSEIGNE DU FAUCHEUR & DU MOUTON

Both gabled buildings were most likely former inns. They were built in the 14th century but razed during the 16th century, so only their ground-floor foundations qualify them as among the oldest houses in Paris. Previous Parisian building regulation codes mandated that timber-framed facades be covered to reduce the risk of fire hazard. Luckily, the added plaster layer was removed during restoration work

conducted in 1967, when André Malraux, the minister of culture at the time, made the Marais a historically protected area. **11 Rue François Miron 75004**

5 FAÇADE OF THE SYNAGOGUE AGOUDAS HAKEHILOS

The Agoudas Hakehilos synagogue was erected in 1913 by the architect Hector Guimard, known for his ornate Art Nouveau structures and his infamous design of the Paris Métro station entrances (original examples of which remain at Porte Dauphine, Abbesses,

and Châtelet). This is the only religious edifice Guimard designed. The venue was commissioned by the Agoudas Hakehilos society, a community of Orthodox Jews of primarily Russian origin who were part of the turn-of-the-20th-century wave of immigration from Eastern Europe. It was registered as a historical monument in 1989. *10 Rue Pavée 75004*

❻ JARDIN DES ROSIERS–
Joseph Migneret

This public garden opened in 2014, uniting several private green spaces at a slight remove from the street. One grassy section faces the Maison de l'Europe, accessible from the Rue des Francs-Bourgeois. The other section is accessible via the Rue des Rosiers, through the entrance of the former Hôtel d'Albret. A large chestnut tree stands at the center, sharing space with dogwoods and orange trees. The park was named in honor of the former director of a nearby school, who was a member of the resistance during World War II and who saved Jewish children from an ugly fate. **10 Rue des Rosiers 75004**

❼ RUE DES ROSIERS:
L'As du Fallafel, Miznon, & Sacha Finkelsztajn

L'As du Fallafel *(number 34)* boasts the "oh-that-must-be-good" winding queues—and sure, you can't go wrong with their chickpea-patty classic heaped with cabbage, cucumbers, and eggplant—but don't discount their (arguably superior) neighbor. The flavorful offerings just around the corner at **Miznon *(22 Rue des Écouffes)*** (an outpost from Tel Avivian chef Eyal Shani) include stuffed pitas with hearty lamb meatballs or *boeuf bourguignon,* and whole-roast-ed vegetables like cauliflower and sweet potatoes. It's noisy and ani-mated and dotted with mounds of fresh vegetables, plus free pita to nibble. For a sweet treat thereafter, find the bright yellow facade of

Sacha Finkelsztajn *(number 27)* (aka La Boutique Jaune), where the cheesecakes, strudels, and linzer tortes draw from storied Eastern European family recipes. **Rue des Rosiers 75004**

8a MUSÉE COGNACQ-JAY GARDEN

The Musée Cognacq-Jay houses the collection of Ernest Cognacq —founder of Parisian department store La Samaritaine (currently under the ownership of LVMH)—and his wife, Marie-Louise Jay. Their trove of 18th-century art, amassed between 1900 and 1927,

was bequeathed to the city. The array is housed in the Hôtel Donon, which maintains a period atmosphere in step with the artworks shown. The museum's main entrance is on Rue Elzévir—but sneak into the petite garden, which is accessible even if you don't want to visit the museum itself. *9 Rue Payenne 75003*

8b INSTITUT SUÉDOIS

Behind the bright blue doors lies a multidisciplinary space celebrating contemporary Swedish culture. Set within the Hôtel de Marle, a mansion built at the end of the 16th century with a grand stair-

case and Louis XVI details, there is a lovely back garden that attracts visitors in the summer. The Café Suédois has *kannelbular* (Swedish cinnamon rolls), tarts, and hot chocolate, which can be enjoyed in the sequestered cobbled courtyard (beware of the avid birds looking for scraps). There are free exhibitions in the gallery space, which has put the spotlight on Swedish creativity, from photography to comic books to craft and textiles. **11 Rue Payenne 75003**

8c SQUARE GEORGES-CAIN

Square Georges-Cain, built in 1923, was named after the painter, writer, and curator of the neighboring Musée Carnavalet. At the garden's epicenter is a bronze statue of a standing female nude by sculptor Aristide Maillol, encircled by greenery and flowers. It's perfect for having lunch if you've grabbed nearby falafel or other tasty bites to go. *8 Rue Payenne 75003*

9 MUSÉE NATIONAL PICASSO & LIBRAIRIE-BOUTIQUE

In October 2015, the Musée National Picasso reopened after a protracted (and fraught) period of remodeling. Picasso, pillar of the art world, needs no introduction to sway a visit of his archive. But as far as gift shops go, this one (designed by French architect Jean-François Bodin) is worth checking out. In addition to information about Picasso's life and work, the shop has a wide assortment of modern and contemporary art reference books. Moreover, the

shelves and tabletops are filled with beautiful objects: Cubist vases, African masks, sketchbooks, tableware, and textiles. *4–5 Rue de Thorigny 75003*

❿ MUSÉE DE LA CHASSE ET DE LA NATURE

The Musée de la Chasse et de la Nature is a private institution highlighting the aesthetics of hunting and nature. Opened in 1967, it was founded by wealthy French industrialist François Sommer and his wife, who were avid hunters and conservationists (their holdings span nearly 3,000 hunting-related objects). The museum, which juxtaposes ancient and contemporary works, is housed within two elegant private mansions, Hôtel de Guénégaud and Hôtel de Mongelas. The thrillingly strange and eclectic collection, which is laid out in a series of fantastical *mise-en-scènes*, includes curio cabinets, taxidermied animals from all continents, 17th-century portraits of Louis XIV's pets, artistic representations of wildlife from tapestries to ceramics to furniture, paintings in naturalistic French Rococo styles—as well as recent works by contemporary European artists. The museum also showcases an array of vintage weaponry from the 16th–19th centuries, including spears, crossbows, and guns once owned by Louis XIII and Napoleon. *62 Rue des Archives 75003*

⓫ RUE VIEILLE DU TEMPLE

A buzzy shopping street, this artery is great for perusing and purchasing. **Breizh Café** *(number 109)* turns out delicious Breton-style buckwheat crêpes and galettes—if the line to sit is long, instead grab a treat to go next door at the **Epicerie Breizh Café** *(number 111)* and eat in the park across the street. Pick up some artisanal French jams, bottles of cider, cans of sardines, or sachets of caramels as gifts

while you're at it. **French Trotters** *(number 128)* is a boutique with a small but careful selection of womenswear and menswear separates, as well as chic footwear and home goods. **Le Slip Français** *(number 137)*—housed in a lovely old building with white-painted vintage beams—sells a French flag palette of red, white, and blue underthings, socks, and swimming garments. Every step of their production is completed in France. *Rue Vieille du Temple 75003*

⓬ MARCHÉ DES ENFANTS ROUGE

Named after an orphanage whose charges wore red garments, the *marché* has been active since 1615. Today, the small marketplace has stalls that sell vegetables and flowers, but it mostly attracts people at mealtimes with its variety of cuisines, all *al fresco*: Japanese bentos, Moroccan stews, saucy Italian specialities, each stand with its own tables for casual, convivial eating. ***39 Rue de Bretagne 75003***

⓭ SQUARE DU TEMPLE – *Elie Wiesel*

Once the location of a state prison (Louis XVI and his family were held there from 1792–1808, during the French Revolution), the square was created in 1857 during the Haussmannian overhaul of the city. Its Second Empire features include a small man-made waterfall cascading onto stones brought in from the forests of Fontainebleau, gates designed by architect Gabriel Davioud, and a gazebo. The nearby Carreau de Temple, a 19th-century glass-and-iron building used for events and sports, was recently renovated. **64 Rue de Bretagne 75003**

⑭ THE BROKEN ARM

This tastemaker concept store—named after a Marcel Duchamp work—is meticulously stocked with both emerging and established fashion designers. Housed in a quiet street of early-20th-century buildings, the store is linked to a bright café, a see-and-be-seen destination beloved by the fashion set for a light lunch. The café's outdoor seating is perfect for people-watching when the weather is fair, with the leafy Square du Temple front row. **12 Rue Perrée 75003**

⑮ JACQUES GENIN

Jacques Genin supplies sweets to more than 200 top French hotels and restaurants, including the Hôtel de Crillon and the Plaza Athénée. Genin does not hold the official *maître chocolatier* title because he built his empire outside the channels of the rigorous French gastronomical system. But no one would doubt the mastery of this self-taught expert, who began his food career in a slaughterhouse and worked as head *pâtissier* at the global chocolate company La Maison du Chocolat. His sweets emporium is a must for any gourmand or chocolate obsessive: be it caramels (in flavors like mango–passion fruit or rhubarb), *pâtes de fruits*, nougats, or *guimauves* (fancy marshmallows). On a cold day, the unctuously thick hot chocolate is not—not!—to be missed.
133 Rue de Turenne 75003

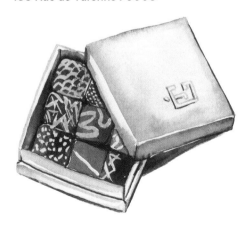

16 CIRQUE D'HIVER

Built in 1852, the Cirque d'Hiver is the oldest circus venue in the world and features a 20-sided polygon of 40 windows. Architect Ignace Jacques Hittorf—who also designed the Gare du Nord—

inaugurated the Second Empire building assisted by painters and sculptors. In 1859, Jules Léotard invented the flying trapeze here, and in 1956, fashion photographer Richard Avedon shot some of his most iconic images with the American model Dovima. Today, count on concerts, light shows, and circus spectacle. **110 Rue Amelot 75011**

⓱ CLOWN BAR

Neither a bar nor a destination for circus folk, this high-end restaurant is thusly named for its proximity to the Cirque d'Hiver. The exquisitely embellished tiled walls behind the bar and painted ceilings do feature clowns. Sven Chartier and Ewen Lemoigne—chefs helming the Parisian restaurant Saturne, a few arrondissements over—created a sophisticated menu and a serious natural wine list, both of which can be enjoyed indoors or on the terrace. A playful surprise: the silverware is kept in secret drawers within the tables themselves. **114 Rue Amelot 75011**

⓲ BOULEVARD BEAUMARCHAIS:
Merci, Bonton, & Maison Plisson

Bonton (*111 Boulevard Beaumarchais*) was created in 2000 by the progeny of the founders of Merci. The cheery shop—for babies and kids (3–12 years old)—makes adults want to revisit their inner child (think: stickers, coloring books, striped straws, bright paper plates). The tiny outfits will rival those of any adult Parisian, and an in-house hairdresser

for kids is also on offer. **Merci (5 Boulevard des Filles du Calvaire)**, a discerning multi-floor boutique accessible through a courtyard, peddles womenswear, menswear, perfume, housewares, stationery, jewelry, glassware, and other stylish goods. It also features whimsi-

cal in-store installations related to design and a chic book-lined café. **Maison Plisson (*93 Boulevard Beaumarchais*)**, launched in 2015, highlights artisans and producers in its two-level *marché/épicerie*. Although significantly smaller scale than New York City's Dean & Deluca, from which it is said to be inspired, it is one of the few food destinations on a stretch populated by clothing stores and vintage camera commerce.

⑲ POLKA GALERIE

Established in 2007, Polka Galerie organizes photography exhibitions in its two spaces—one located in a prettily cobbled courtyard removed from the street. The venue is linked to the quarterly *Polka Magazine,* which explores the vitality of photography production and practices, both contemporary and historical. **12 Rue Saint-Gilles 75003**

⑳ PLACE DES VOSGES

Spearheaded by King Henry IV in 1605 and christened La Place Royale, Place de Vosges was renamed by Napoleon as a nod to the first region in the country (Vosges) that forked over taxes to the revolutionary government. This serene space has four symmetrical fountains and a statue of Louis XIII at the center, hemmed in on all sides by beautiful brick-and-stone facades and chestnut trees. Its arcades house cafés as well as author Victor Hugo's former abode (he of *Les Misérables* and *The Hunchback of Notre-Dame* fame)—which is now a museum. This Place is one of the few spaces where visitors are allowed to sprawl on the grass: on a sunny day, green space is covered with teenagers laying about, children toddling around, and elders watching from the benches. **Place des Vosges 75004**

HOW TO *Apero*

WHAT IS AN APÉRO?

"L'apéro" is short for "l'apéritif," a pre-dinner drink enjoyed from 6–9 p.m. (ish). The casual and beloved ritual—like the Italian *aperitivo*—is a starting point to the night with a built-in social component. Sometimes it's just a quick drink accompanied by olives or peanuts; sometimes it's a languorous slew of hours of drinking, accompanied by small plates (cheese, charcuterie—pretty much anything finger food–esque that's easy to nibble) prior to dinner. Cocktails, beer, and wines are staples of this drinking ritual, but—this being France—wine takes the lead.

ON NATURAL WINE

The burgeoning natural wine movement *(vin nature)* in France has been especially exciting in recent years. Natural wine is made without chemicals and minimum technological intervention, a throwback that predates the industrialization of the wine-making and bottling process. The "natural" aspect is ultimately a hands-off, let-nature-be-great approach: in regard to both the growing of the grapes (organically, without pesticides) and the pressing of the grapes (without intervening with some form of chemical manipulation, barring an occasional tiny quantity of sulfites).

The codes of the natural wine industry are hard to pinpoint because practices differ from producer to producer (winemakers disagree widely about "acceptable" levels of intervention). However, some basic criteria tends to be generally accepted: the use of organically or biodynamically grown grapes (with or without certification), the maintenance of low-yielding vineyards that are hand-picked, a refusal to add sugars/yeasts/bacteria/additives for color or flavor, minimal or no filtration, and minimal or no added sulfites. In this way, the unique aspects of the local French *terroir* transfer their distinctive features to the grapes: the environment, the season, and methods of production.

5 NATURAL WINE SPECIALISTS

Le Garde Robe
41 Rue de l'Arbre Sec 75001

La Cave du Paul Bert
16 Rue Paul Bert 75011

Le Verre Volé
38 Rue Oberkampf 75011

Le Siffleur de Ballons
34 Rue de Cîteaux 75012

La Cave des Papilles
35 Rue Daguerre 75014

WINE VOCABULARY TO KNOW

Cave: wine cellar

Cave à manger: wine bar where food is available (or sometimes required)

Caviste: wine merchant

Terroir: particular natural environment in which a wine is produced, influenced by soil, topography, and climate

Verre: a glass

Vigneron: wine-grower

Centre 1ST ARRONDISSEMENT

Starting point:
PALAIS-ROYAL

PLACE VENDÔME

RUE DANIELLE CASANOVA

RUE DE RICHELIEU

RUE VIVIENNE

RUE SAINT-ANNE

RUE DES PETITS CHAMPS

RUE DES PYRAMIDES

2B

2C

2A

2

RUE SAINT-HONORE

DU MONT THABOR

RUE D'ALGER

3

AVENUE DE L'OPERA

1C

1B

1A

RUE DE VALOIS

(M) 7 14

5

1

4

(M) 1

RUE SAINT ROCH

RUE DE RIVOLI

(M) 1

6

AVENUE DU GENERAL LEMMONIER

8

RUE SAINT-HON

RUE DE RIVOLI

7

PLACE DU CARROUSEL

RUE CROIX DES PETIT

PONT ROYALE

PONT DU CARROUSEL

QUAI DES TUILERIES

QUAI VOLTAIRE

The heart of the city brims with iconic museums and architectural classicism. The Tuileries is the city's epicenter: its axis determined the planning of the grand Avenue des Champs Elysées, thanks to landscaper André le Nôtre. The Avenue still provides an incredible sense of perspective, a linear logic that isn't always visible in Paris, where winding haphazard streets built during various eras often come together in a patchwork. Moreover, the Tuileries are bookended from all corners by some of the richest art collections in the world.

Nearby, the Palais-Royal is the tranquil counterpart to the feverish frenzy of tourists in the Tuileries; its old-world charm remains, even as luxury commerce encircles it. The patrimonial mixes surprisingly well with the adjacent Japanese quarter, full of noodle soup restaurants and Asian groceries.

1 PALAIS-ROYAL

Encircled by high-end boutiques (Rick Owens, Stella McCartney, Acne), the Palais-Royal is at once a chic and calm destination, neatly trimmed with trees. Designed by architect Jacques Lemercier, who also designed the Sorbonne, the Palais-Royal was initially the personal residence of Cardinal Richelieu. Thereafter, it was a royal residence, then from 1661 the seat of the Orléans family. Today, it houses the Council of State and Ministry of Culture. The stunning arcades that edge the garden play with shadow and perspective, and the area boasts long-standing public theaters: the Théâtre du Palais-Royal and the Comédie-Française, both designed by Victor Louis during the 18th century. The courtyard closest to the Rue Saint-Honoré features Daniel Buren's site-specific 1986 installation *Les Deux Plateaux (Les Colonnes de Buren),* where kids scamper between striped columns and tourists take playful photos. Finding an available green chair around the central fountain, be it for reading or tanning or eating lunch, is practically a competitive sport on a sunny day. **Place du Palais-Royal 75001**

1a

SERGE LUTENS

Behind the automatic door is a black and violet palette: paneled walls with moons and suns, a starry ceiling, a spiral staircase, and an olfactory spectrum of musk, cedar, amber, and vanilla. Serge Lutens had been powdering and painting the Paris fashion set since the 1960s when he started collaborating on makeup looks with *Vogue, Elle, Harper's Bazaar,* and Christian Dior. In 2000, Lutens created his brand of namesake perfumes and makeup. His fragrances sound as poetic as the aromas they emit: Ambre Sultan, Tubéreuse Criminelle, Cuir Mauresque, Nuit de Cellophane, Fille de Berlin... **142 Galerie de Valois 75001**

❶ DIDIER LUDOT

This *dépôt-vente de luxe,* founded in 1975, is a happy hunting spot for lovers of vintage luxury womenswear and menswear. The displays on Stockman mannequins are overhung with bright red lampshades. There is '90s Lacroix, '80s Alaia, '70s Balmain, and '60s Nina Ricci. Chanel T-straps neighbor Hermès cuff links, Fendi bags neighbor Manolo Blahnik wedges—and that's in the front vitrine alone.
24 Galerie de Montpensier 75001

1c
CAFÉ KITSUNÉ

Formerly a tiny showroom for textiles, this coffee counter has few seated spots inside, but great outdoor seating for ringside people-watching. Grab a latte—matcha or otherwise—and a gluten-free sweet and make your way into the park. The Kitsuné boutique, which sells ready-to-wear and accessories (like a baseball cap stitched with the word *Parisien*), is around the corner. **51 Galerie de Montpensier 75001**

2 GALERIE VIVIENNE

Galerie Vivienne is one of a handful of covered passages in the city center. Inaugurated in 1826, it is based on plans drawn up by the architect François-Jean Delannoy, whose neoclassical decor and Italianate mosaics are overhung with an elegant canopy. The glazed rotunda is decorated with nymphs. Strolling these halls becomes a thrillingly regressive immersion into 19th-century Paris—despite the contemporary shops, one can easily envision the bustling commerce of the past. **Galerie Vivienne 75002**

② BOUGAINVILLE

As with the Galerie Vivienne itself, this bar has a "what time period am I in?" feel, if perhaps not quite so receded. There's the copper bar, the yellow Formica, the speckled tiled floor, the wide picture windows, plus covered outdoor seating directly in the passage itself. If the venue looks a tad shabby, it only speaks to the no-frills attitude of its solid classical bistro cuisine, paired with a robust natural wine list (at unrivaled prices). **5 Rue de la Banque 75002**

2b SI TU VEUX

Here are toys that beckon to adults and children alike: a cross-generational selection. There are natural wood blocks from Poland, plastic boat bath toys from Germany, plus stuffed bears, masks, balloons, tops, tiny cars, and construction sets. The doll-size fake food, like cans of peas or a tiny tub of Nutella, are perfect for the budding household chef. Many of the games and toys are inspired by the Montessori School approach, although the store is not overtly branded as such. **68 Galerie Vivienne 75002**

2c DAROCO

Jean Paul Gaultier's former boutique on Rue Vivienne was transformed into a sprawling two-level trattoria. With 190 seats and a cocktail bar, the trattoria is open seven days a week and the staff is outfitted in striped maritime garb, a wink to Gaultier's signature "Hello, Sailor!" vibe. Cavernous by French standards, with green marble and mirrors, the open kitchen delivers wood-fired pizzas (the margherita is made with *fior di latte* and tomatoes from Mezzogiorno), and rustic *linguine alla carbonara*. Sip it all down with prosecco, red wine from Sardinia, white wine from Abruzzo—or hit the dedicated bar, tucked in the back with a view of the Galerie Vivienne, for apéritifs or after-dinner drinks. It's one of the few Parisian venues with nonstop service from noon until midnight. **6 Rue Vivienne 75002**

❸ RESTAURANT KUNITORAYA & UDON BISTROT KUNITORAYA

This headquarters for hand-pulled udon noodles (house-made from Japanese wheat flour) has two adjacent venues. Restaurant Kunitoraya is the most recent and more casual—you can usually spot the line restlessly waiting from the street. Long and narrow, with an open kitchen, the entrance gives way to communal table seating backgrounded by raw brick. The servers, dressed in nurse white, work briskly, undercutting the tendency of French diners to linger over a meal for hours.

Udon Bistrot Kunitoraya, the fancier sister down the street (reservation required), is a singular hybrid of the French-Japanese experience. The venue evokes the turn-of-the-century Parisian brasserie (zinc, mirrors, white ceramic tiling) but with a soigné Japanese touch. There's a heavy wooden bar at the entrance; the kitchen is in the recesses. It serves an *à la carte* lunch and a *menu dégustation* (tasting menu) for dinner, including a succession of tempura, hot or cold udon, a char-grilled main, and dessert. ***1 Rue Villedo and 5 Rue Villedo 75001***

④ ASTIER DE VILLATTE

Astier de Villatte has long distinguished itself for its 18th- and 19th-century-inspired pottery. Using a black terra-cotta base, each item is finished with a white glaze that highlights the unique character of the clay. The boutique doubles as a dreamy rustic country house, with chevron wood floors and vintage display cases. There are carefully piled serving plates and scalloped bowls, signature patterned notebooks by a one-of-a-kind typographer, and incense sticks that conjure far-flung travel (Delhi, Villa Medici). The designs span bourgeois dinner platters to Charlie Brown–shaped candle lids. In collaboration with John Derian, a housewares maven based in New York, the two labels create joint new designs biannually, featuring painted whimsical iconography like whales or mushrooms. ***173 Rue Saint-Honoré 75001***

❺ SAINT-ROCH

The Église Saint-Roch is known as a *paroisse des artistes,* or parish for artists: it has been a spiritual refuge for French cultural icons such as the playwright Molière, philosopher Denis Diderot, and fashion designer Yves Saint Laurent. Its construction began in 1653—adolescent Louis XIV symbolically laid the first stone—resulting in baroque architectural beauty. If the facade and nave remain classical, the chapel is an extremely theatrical showcase of splendor: Three organs, sculptures, and paintings. ***296 Rue Saint-Honoré 75001***

❻ JARDIN DES TUILERIES

This sprawling garden, located between the Louvre and the Place de la Concorde, is so-called because the area was once full of workshops making roof tiles, or *tuileries.* In the 16th century, Catherine de Medici

commissioned a landscaper to model the gardens of the Tuileries palace on those of her native Florence. A century later, the landscape architect André Le Nôtre was commissioned for a redesign. (Le Nôtre was, in fact, the grandson of one of Catherine de Medici's gardeners.) He transformed the Tuileries into a garden *à la française,* implementing a style based on symmetry and long perspectives, a signature he developed at Vaux-le-Vicomte and Versailles. It became a public park after the French Revolution.

At the beginning of the 20th century, the Tuileries garden was filled with entertainment—puppet theaters, toy boat basins, donkey rides, toy sellers—until interrupted by World War I. During the 1960s, André Malraux, the then-minister of culture, removed ancient statues and replaced them with contemporary sculptures by

Aristide Maillol. In the late 1990s, new sculptures by Jean Dubuffet, Henry Moore, and Auguste Rodin were sprinkled in; in 2000, works by living artists—including Louise Bourgeois, Roy Lichtenstein, Giuseppe Penone, and Lawrence Weiner—were added. In the 21st century, French landscape architects Pascal Cribier and Louis Benech have been working to restore some of the features of André Le Nôtre's original concept. **Place de la Concorde 75001**

Museums

7 The **Musée du Louvre** is a historic monument and staple landmark: it spans 38,000 objects on view, culled from prehistory to the 21st century. The Louvre Palace was originally intended as a fortress to protect the city from possible Viking attacks in the late 12th century. In 1546, it became the main residence of French kings; in 1682, Louis XIV switched his household to Versailles, leaving it primarily as a display for the royal collection. It opened as a museum in 1793, with an exhibition of works confiscated from the royals and the church. During World War II, the museum removed most of the art and hid valuable pieces. The institution has weathered controversies surrounding cultural property and appropriation—for works seized under Napoleon I, as well as those seized by the Nazis—and has participated in arbitration sessions with UNESCO. The collection is divided into eight curatorial departments, from Egyptian Antiquities to Islamic Art to Prints and Drawings.

There are two satellite Louvre museums: one in the French town

of Lens, and one in Abu Dhabi. *Three entrances—via Pyramid and Galerie du Carrousel, Passage Richelieu, or Porte des Lions.*

8 The **Musée des Arts Décoratifs (Museum of Decorative Arts),** located in the Palais du Louvre's western wing, hosts regularly rotating temporary exhibitions on fashion, advertising, design, and graphic arts. Amongst its vast and stunning permanent collections, the museum displays furniture and interiors, *objets d'arts*, tapestries, wallpaper, porcelain, ceramics, glassware, and toys. There are numerous immersive rooms in the Art Nouveau and Art Deco styles, with a full recreation of designer Jeanne Lanvin's sumptuous house, decorated by Albert-Armand Rateau in the early 1920s. *107 Rue de Rivoli 75001*

9 The **Jeu de Paume,** a hub of photography and multimedia exhibitions, is located in the northwestern corner of the Tuileries. It originally housed real tennis courts—*jeu de paume* is a game that predated tennis—and its quea-

sier legacy is that it was used from 1940 to 1944 by the Nazi-annexed regime in France to store looted collections from Jewish families and "degenerate" art banned from entering Germany. From the *après-guerre* until the 1980s, the museum held important Impressionist works now housed in the Musée d'Orsay. A 1989 renovation yielded a spacious three-floor exhibition space and a windowed atrium flooded with natural light, with views onto the gardens as well as Place de la Concorde and the tip of the Eiffel Tower. Since 2004, there have been survey exhibitions on greats such as Taryn Simon, Garry Winogrand, Lorna Simpson, Philippe Halsman, Cindy Sherman, Martin Parr, Helena Almeida, Berenice Abbott, André Kertész, and more. **1 Place de la Concorde 75008**

⑩ The **Musée de l'Orangerie,** located in the southwest corner of the Tuileries, features Impressionist and post-Impressionist paintings. The Orangerie was designed in 1852 by the architect Firmin Bourgeois to shelter the orange trees planted in the garden. The

venue has had many lives: under the Third Republic it was used as a deposit for goods, as an examination room, and as housing for mobilized soldiers; it also hosted sporting, musical, and patriotic events. Artist Claude Monet donated his sumptuous *Nymphéas* (Water Lilies) series to the French government, housed—contractually—in the institution's oval rooms. In a setting characterized by natural light and sparse interiors, his eight paintings were made available for public viewing in 1927. Though Monet's work has become synonymous with the museum, there are also notable works by Paul Cézanne, Henri Matisse, Amedeo Modigliani, Pablo Picasso, and Pierre-Auguste Renoir, in addition to regularly rotating exhibitions of painting and photography. ***Jardin de Tuileries (on the side of the River Seine) 7500***

11 The **Musée d'Orsay** on the left bank of the Seine is housed in the former Gare d'Orsay, a Beaux-Arts railway station built at the turn of the twentieth century. Constructed for the 1900 *Exposition Universelle,* the station was redesigned as a museum by ACT Architecture; Gae Aulenti imagined the interior layout, decoration, and fittings. In 1986, the museum officially opened with mainly French art dating from 1848 to 1914. It houses the largest collection of Impressionist and post-Impressionist masterpieces in the world. The Musée d'Orsay clock in the main hall is one of its iconographic lynchpins. ***1 Rue de la Légion d'Honneur 75007***

Belleville & Buttes-Chaumont

19TH & 20TH ARRONDISSEMENTS

Starting point:
MÉTRO
COLONEL
FABIEN

The northeastern hills of Paris are often exempt from the tourism "musts" list. It's a relief for the locals, no doubt, but a detriment to experiencing the diverse riches of the city. The Belleville area is a confluence: a Chinatown (smaller than the one in the 13th arrondissement, though also heavily scented by the distinctive durian fruit), a home to a Jewish community and its kosher markets, and a North African community selling honeyed Tunisian sweets and hallal meats. The ramshackle neighborhood—although gentrification-adjacent—remains relatively populaire, or working class. This is offset by emerging galleries, artist ateliers, and bars, which pepper streets on and off of the central Rue de Belleville that divides the 19th and 20th arrondissements. While Chinese dumplings and Thai soups prevail, a new wave of small plates-and-natural wine bars are starting to crop up. Further atop the hills are unsung views that rival those in the more de facto heights of the 18th arrondissement. Here, green space is deployed much more accessibly than in the manicured parks in the city center—there are few admonishments to keep off the grass. As small businesses start looking this way, the future of this urban area is sure to evolve in the coming years.

❶ PCF (PARTI COMMUNIST FRANÇAIS) HEADQUARTERS

The Communist headquarters is located off the roundabout on the Place du Colonel Fabien. Behind the white spaceship-esque dome,

which rises from the undulating courtyard, is a sinuous building with smoked-glass windows and steel-and-aluminum frames resting upon a concrete base. The components were designed by Brazilian architect Oscar Niemeyer in 1965 and classified as a historical monument in 2007. (Niemeyer—who drew up Brazil's modernist capital, Brasília, and worked with Le Corbusier on the United Nations headquarters in New York—was himself a committed Communist.) The main hall offers rotating artistic exhibitions, and the venue has been rented out to organizations to raise financial resources for the party (an architect's office, a design studio, and a production company work out of there). The venue is also rented to film crews and for Paris fashion week, with Prada, Thom Browne, and Jean Paul Gaultier having held *défilés* there previously. ***2 Place du Colonel Fabien 75019***

❷ BUTTE BERGEYRE

Deemed a *"micro-quartier,"* this charming, discreet, and wholly residential pocket is situated on a hill to the west of the Buttes-Chaumont park. Stretching about 330 feet (100 m) in altitude above the street, this area can be spotted via perplexing clues: stairs that seem to lead into the sky, a hallucinatory stretch of lush pinot noir vines *(Clos des Chaufourniers)* planted between blocky buildings.

From the Rue Georges-Lardennois, the butte provides a panoramic view of northern Paris, notably of Montmartre and Sacré-Cœur.

The Butte Bergeyre was formerly a stadium, although a short-lived one. Inaugurated in 1918 and destroyed in 1926, it is named for rugby player Robert Bergeyre. Creative figures have resided in these environs at different times (including artist Jean-Paul Goude, director Jacques Audiard, and designer Marc Newson). The area was photographed by Willy Ronis in the 1950s, filmed by Michel Gondry for his adaptation of a Boris Vian novel, and used as a setting for contemporary French author Virginie Despentes. Among the many architectural delights, keep an eye out for the strange Maison Zilveli, designed by Modernist Jean Welz, flanking the hill on concrete pillars. **Rue Georges Lardennois 75019**

❸ BUTTES-CHAUMONT

The Buttes-Chaumont, the fifth-largest Parisian park, opened in 1867 to coincide with Paris's 1869 *Exposition Universelle*. It was an unlikely site: due to the chemical composition of its soil, it was almost bare of vegetation (in fact it was dubbed Chauve-mont, or "bald hill"). Zoned outside the city limits until 1860, the park had a sinister rep until the middle of 18th century: criminals were hanged there and left to dangle. After the 1789 revolution, it became a dump, a cemetery for horse carcasses, then a sewage depository. Another part of the site was a gypsum and limestone quarry, mined for construction materials. It was Baron Haussmann who designated it to be a new public park to entertain the rapidly growing populace. Work began in 1864, under the direction of Jean-Charles Alphand, who oversaw all the major parks at the time, including the Bois de Boulogne and the Bois de Vincennes. It took two years simply to terrace the land, and explosives were used to sculpt the buttes into dramati-

cally jagged cliffs. Hydraulic pumps funneled in water from the canal to create a picturesque waterfall. Trees, flowers, and grasses were planted, turning it into a natural sanctuary.

The main park entrance is at Place Armand-Carrel, though there are other access points into the park, as well as around the perimeter. Once inside amid the greenery, expect a slew of Lycra-clad runners, leisurely dog-walkers, and bride-and-groom photo shoots (the 19th arrondissement *mairie,* or town hall, is nearby). On sunny weekends, the sloping lawns are a visual cacophony of sunbathers and picknickers, so numerous as to almost mask the grasses entirely. The park currently hosts three bars (Pavillon du Lac, Pavillon Puebla, Rosa Bonheur) and also has a guignol theater. ***Avenue Mathurin Moreau 75019***

③ₐ ÎLE DU BELVÉDÈRE & TEMPLE DE LA SIBYLLE

Perhaps the most famous feature of the park is the Temple de la Sibylle, completed in 1867. Perched atop the Île du Belvédère, an 165-foot (50-m) cliff fashioned from the former gypsum quarry, the

structure overlooks an artificial lake below. It was inspired by the ancient Temple of Vesta in Italy—the subject of many 17th- to 19th-century landscape paintings—and articulated here at a miniature scale. Gabriel Davioud, the city's chief architect under Napoleon III, designed this, as well as the park's belvederes, rain shelters, gatehouses, and fences (made of *trompe l'oeil* cement "logs"). Davioud's rustic style was inspired not only by ancient Rome, but also the chalets and bridges of the Swiss Alps.

Parc des Buttes-Chaumont 75019

③b ROSA BONHEUR

A contemporary version of the traditional *guinguette*—a lively dance-hall bar where locals gathered—Rosa Bonheur is named after the successful 19th-century French artist and sculptor. Although the venue has ample outdoor seating, the summertime queues are for real so arrive early. It is a hub of raucous good fun in warm weather and also hosts regular gay nights. *Parc des Buttes-Chaumont, 2 Allée de la Cascade 75019*

④ LE PLATEAU

This exhibition space, launched in 2002, hosts multidisciplinary exhibitions of contemporary emerging artists (lots of video pieces!) as well as a program of collaborative performing arts events. The space is part of the Frac Île-de-France network, which supports and collects contemporary art, displaying the works in their network of venues throughout the country. Entrance is free.

22 Rue des Alouettes 75019

⑤ RUE DE LA VILLETTE

This street has not a shred of cosmopolitan cool—and that's a compliment. Stretching from Rue de Belleville to the Parc des

Buttes-Chaumont, the village vibe is what makes it so endearing. There's a series of small shops: an atypical hairdresser-florist, a pastel-hued spot that hosts ateliers for kids, the dreamy Villa l'Adour (a blue-gated private cobbled way of houses with colored shutters), an Italian eatery offering pasta Pugliese and burrata with rucola, and small boutiques with local designers and second-hand items. Stop at the corner bar Chacun Fait for a beer in the sun. *Rue de la Villette 75019*

❻ Ô DIVIN

This trifecta of comestibles has completely upped the gastronomy game in the neighborhood. There's no better place to get picnic-equipped. At **Epicerie Ô Divin** *(number 130),* grab a bottle of

natural wine or Deck & Donohue craft beers, caper berries, Kalamata olives, sausages, rillettes, or rabbit terrines. Then pop next door to the primeur **(number 128)** to have a look at the market selection of seasonal fruit and vegetables, as well as cheeses, procured straight from small French producers. There are always some exotic extras: from wild garlic (ail des ours) to black radish to rhizomes of turmeric. At the traiteur **(number 118),** there is a rotating daily selection of prepared foods and fresh salads, available to go or on-site. Outside the joint is a rotisserie unit where you are likely to find a whole pig roasting on a spit (cochon de lait) or a whole chicken—heads included. **Rue de Belleville 75020**

❼ ÉGLISE SAINT JEAN–BAPTISTE DE BELLEVILLE

This neo-Gothic church was designed by Jean-Baptiste-Antoine Lassus, one of the first to deploy this architectural style in mid-19th-century France. Lassus was known for overseeing the restoration of considerable monuments like Sainte-Chapelle and Notre-Dame. Lassus also taught Eugène Viollet-le-Duc (the architect and theorist later hired to design the internal structure of the Statue of Liberty). Here, he designed the structure and furnishings, with outside help

for the stained-glass windows and forged ironwork. In 2014, when the city required the church to bring its electrical system up to standard, it installed striking LED-lit chandeliers.

139 Rue de Belleville 75019

❽ VIEW OF THE EIFFEL TOWER

In truth, this location is not at all glamorous, but it still delivers a great perspective! Across from the McDonald's and adjacent to the Metro station at Pyrénées, position yourself in front of the kebab window to get a diagonal glimpse at Gustave Eiffel's monumental icon. *92 Rue de Belleville 75020*

❾ BUGADA & CARGNEL

Few spaces in the area's emerging Belleville gallery scene rival this one. Founded by Claudia Cargnel and Frédéric Bugada in 2002, this vast airy venue was once a garage—as such, the blending of the doorway into the slatted portal makes it very easy to miss. The luminous high-ceilinged space, built in the 1930s, is overhung by a glass roof. The gallery represents French and international emerging artists like Cyprien Gaillard, Iris Van Dongen, Théo Mercier, and Pierre Bismuth. *7 Rue de l'Equerre 75019*

❿ PARC DE BELLEVILLE

Conceived by architect François Debulois and landscaper Paul Brichet, this green space was inaugurated in 1988. Until the 18th century, Belleville was not part of Paris, just countryside with farms, windmills, and open-air cafés. People of modest means lived there, chased out of Paris by Haussmann's renovations at the end of the 19th century. At its highest point, the Parc de Belleville provides an unbeatable panoramic view of the city: you can easily spot the Centre Georges Pompidou, Notre-Dame, the Pantheon, École Militaire, and the Eiffel Tower in a single horizon line. At sun-

down, the sky's fluorescence contrasts beautifully with Paris's gray rooftops. *7 Rue Piat 75020*

⑪ CAFÉ BELLEVILLE

The crew behind Parisian roastery Belleville Brûlerie, and old school–style café La Fontaine de Belleville, have expanded their caffeinated energy with a buzzy coffee shop. Past the retractable street-side vitrine, the frontal coffee counter all but bursts onto Rue de Belleville. The space is flecked with touches of terrazzo, marble, and copper, and dotted with vivacious plant greenery. With several *café du jour* options, one can gulp back an espresso at the counter *(à la française)*, or take a to-go cup *(à la expat)*, or grab a table on-site along the wraparound woven banquette. When the weather's nice, hit the terrace that extends into Place Fréhel, over which hang

huge frescoes made by French artists Jean Le Gac and Ben Vautier. *50 Rue de Belleville 75019*

⑫ CAVE DE BELLEVILLE

The cavernous bottle shop has wooden structures neatly lined with wine at its entrance. Beyond that is seating for in-house dining and drinking, with a communal table under a pretty archway in the back. Close to the Parc de Belleville, it's the no-brainer for grabbing something when you plan to sit and drink hillside (ask them to insta-chill your bottle). The *épicerie* in the front sells Moliterno truffle cheese and chorizo Iberico for a complete picnic. Or stay in: there's a selection of wine served by the glass, and platters of charcuterie and cheese, and artisanal canned goods opened on the spot (razor clams, mussels *à l'escabèche*, sardines in olive oil). *51 Rue de Belleville 75019*

⑬ GUO XIN

This small Chinese eatery gets jam-packed quickly, and its popularity is understandable: the food is that miraculous combination of cheap and tasty. With red lanterns as the only decorative flourish, this is not a place to go for the atmosphere—but who cares when there's a greasy food craving that can be sated. Dip pork-and-chive dumplings (they're deemed *"raviolis"* in French) in black vinegar and chili oil, and be sure to order the sautéed aubergines off the list of vegetable sides. Service is brisk but efficient. Get in early or late, since space is limited. *47 Rue de Belleville 75019*

⓮ AUX FOLIES

Once a cabaret, today this local café is open morning until night, transforming itself over the course of the day to reflect its different populations. The early regulars, who read newspapers with cheap bitter coffee, turn into afternoon idlers with beers at *apéro*. The neon-red lettering is evocative of a David Lynch film and makes for a lively scene at night all the way until closing. The terrace remains packed in summer and winter alike (somehow enough rickety plastic chairs materialize and the contours of the terrace spread amorphously). A low-key but veritable institution, Aux Folies is the perfect place to watch the diversity of Belleville in full force: *habitués* living in the neighborhood and visiting internationals, a wondrous mélange of generations and origins. Everyone is exchanging lighters and ordering cheap, free-flowing beer while local characters—a guy aggressively selling peanuts, homeless people looking for cigarettes—make appearances. The service is swift and friendly despite the crowds. **8 Rue de Belleville 75020**

⑮ RUE DÉNOYEZ

Tucked in along a cobbled side street, Rue Dénoyez (*noyer* means "to drown"—and crazily enough there's a public swimming pool on the street) is a palimpsest of graffiti. You're more likely to come across a street artist here than a car. The laneway is a vibrant slice of street culture and zany *ateliers d'artistes* that use walls and windows as an open-air canvas. Lately, the street has become a magnet for new restaurants offering delicious market menus and natural wine—**Le Désnoyez** and **Le Grand Bain** are musts, selling elegant plates in welcoming decors, without compromising the shabby vibrancy of their neighbors. **3 Rue Dénoyez and 14 Rue Denoyez 75020**

⑯ LA COMMUNE

Punch bowls are usually a no-frills solution at forgettable parties—but not so here! There's no exterior sign, but look for the clear modular screens hiding a jungle plant-speckled terrace with cozy armchairs and a polished minimalist interior. From the same team of exacting cocktail specialists who created Le Syndicat, in the 10th arrondissement, here they mix exquisite concoctions using cognac, Calvados, Corsican brandy, or elderflower liqueur, paired with ingredients such as lemongrass, Indian red tea, fresh lemons, Jamaican pepper, fresh coriander, and homemade syrups. The punch is served in beautiful silver and copper vintage bowls, with stirrers, which can sustain groups ranging from two to ten people. *80 Blvd. de Belleville 75020*

⑰ CAFÉ CHÉRI(E)

With its sticky countertop and free chips, this red-painted dive bar attracts a young crowd craving afternoon sunshine, including students from the nearby school of architecture, and local regulars. The happy hour has well-priced pints, and the sidewalk terrace—where red plastic chairs face out in rows like a classroom—directly faces the sun, allowing for excellent urban tanning. On weekend nights there's a DJ pumping cheesy tunes, with packed-in people dancing like mad. *44 Blvd. de la Villette 75019*

⓲ RUE SAINTE-MARTHE

Built in the 19th century, Sainte-Marthe housed one of the first sets of workers' residences in the capital. Today, it's charming and full of colorful character, quiet during the day and lively in the evening—the Place Sainte-Marthe is hidden within a network of narrow streets. With laundry draped in the windows, it evokes a Mediterranean spot like Naples or Marseilles. The bright facades include bistros, artists' studios, and a record store. ***Rue Sainte-Marthe 75010***

⓳ CAVE À MICHEL

This informal wine bar—a narrow, standing-room-only joint—hosts a discerning crowd who squeeze in to drink from the natural wine list and sophisticated, small plate–sized delicacies turned out in the tiny open kitchen at the end of the bar. The place is under the stewardship of chef Romain Tischenko, who also presides in the kitchen at neighboring sit-down restaurant Le Galopin. *36 Rue Sainte-Marthe 75010*

⓴ LA TÊTE DANS LES OLIVES

Cédric Casanova is the olive oil merchant for some of the most celebrated Parisian restaurants (notably Septime). This pocket-sized slice of Sicily is a high-quality delicatessen by day (seasonal ingredients range from blood oranges to pink garlic) and a tiny restaurant after opening hours (be sure to book months in advance). Dinner sessions serve a group of six diners only, seated at a fold-out communal table in the middle of the shop, surrounded by crates and jars. It's BYOB, and the meal itself will depend on the season and the host's current Mediterranean-flecked inspiration. *2 Rue Sainte-Marthe 75010*

HOW TO HANDLE THE
Cheese Counter

Skip the supermarket and head to
a specialized *fromager*, or cheese monger.
Don't hesitate to ask to sample before buying.

You can't go wrong with these 3 classics:

COMTÉ Made from unpasteurized cow's milk in the Jura Massif/
Franche-Comté region, this cheese is produced in flat discs, yielding pale yellow with a brown rind. The texture is firm yet flexible, the
taste mild but fruity. The manufacture of Comté has been AOC
regulated since 1958, which requires using milk only from Montbé-
liarde cattle nourished with natural feed and grazed in pastures with
limited fertilization. The date of production must be labeled, to trace
the maturing for a minimum of four months, then ripened up to 18
or 24 months. Its ability to melt easily means Comté is ideal for
fondues and *croque monsieur* sandwiches.

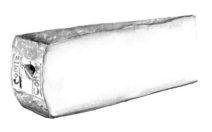

CHÉVRE Made for thousands of years by allowing raw milk to naturally curdle, then draining and pressing the curds, goat cheese is probably one of the longest-standing dairy products. It is often brined during the aging process so it will form a rind, and is then stored for several months to cure. The Loire Valley and Poitou produce a great number of goat's-milk cheeses. Examples of French *chèvres* include the Bucheron, Chabis, Chavroux, Crottin de Chavignol, Faisselle, Pélardon, and Pyramide.

CAMEMBERT A soft, creamy cow's-milk cheese, the first Camembert was made from unpasteurized milk from Normandes cows. The curd is cut roughly into cubes, salted, and transferred to low cylindrical molds, turned every few hours to allow the whey to drain evenly. After 48 hours, each mold contains a flat, cylindrical mass; the cheeses are left to ripen for a (legally required) minimum of three

weeks, yielding an edible rind and creamy interior. Brie is a similar soft cheese, also made from cow's milk; however, it originates from the Île de France region and is ripened more slowly than the Camembert, yielding a slightly milder taste.

Ménilmontant, 75020

Originally a hamlet within an independent municipality, Ménilmontant was, like other communes surrounding the capital, absorbed into the city limits in 1860. Long a working-class neighborhood, Ménilmontant features panoramic views down the barrel of its large hill, and narrow streets that feel like an anachronistic version of French urban life. Ménilmontant was the setting of the classic Palme d'Or-winning French short film, The Red Balloon (1956)—charmingly enough, the area hasn't changed a great deal!

LE MONT EN L'AIR

 Sequestered just below the main drag of Rue de Ménilontant, this bookstore sells literature, fanzines, graphic novels, art and design books, plus a dedicated children's section. **2 Rue de la Mare 75020**

LE PERCHOIR

Two words: huge rooftop. The street entrance is unmarked, but once you take the elevator to the top floor, a 360-degree view of the capital unfolds. Get there early as there are queues—everyone wants to see the sunset over Paris, obviously. **14 Rue Crespin du Gast 75011**

LA FINE MOUSSE

 An artisanal beer bar, serving both *bière française* and international options, offers 20 diverse options on tap that change regularly. Drink up at the long L-shaped bar, or duck into the leather seats against the stone wall. **4 bis Avenue Jean Aicard 75011**

ÉGLISE NOTRE-DAME-DE-LA-CROIX

This neo-Roman/neo-Gothic structure was completed in 1880 under the architect Louis-Jean-Antoine Héret. The lovely, towering edifice in the middle of Place de Ménilmontant somehow remains relatively inconspicuous in its humble environs. **3 Place de Ménilmontant 75020**

LES TROIS 8
This bar's punky vibe belies its sophisticated selection of artisanal beers (eight on tap), plus a wide selection of bottled beers and a few natural wines. The charcuterie-and-cheese boards are excellent and copious, handed over unceremoniously with an uncut half-baguette to rip into, plus jars of cornichons and jam for garnishing. **11 Rue Victor Letalle 75020**

LA BELLEVILLOISE
Founded in 1877, La Bellevilloise was the first Parisian cooperative, enabling those of modest means access to a political and cultural education. In 2005, it reopened as an artistic venue hosting concerts, a club, and a restaurant. In good weather, have a drink on the back terrace and get an eyeful of the charming 20th arrondissement rooftops. **19–21 Rue Boyer 75020**

PÈRE LACHAISE CEMETERY
The largest cemetery in Paris, this thrillingly macabre hotbed of former cultural icons contains Oscar Wilde's tomb plus the headstones of playwright Molière, composer Chopin, Doors lead singer Jim Morrison, and the writer Colette. **16 Rue du Repos 75020**

LA BUVETTE
At this *cave à manger*, the excellent natural wines are complemented by a perfect selection of small plates (fat white beans with lemon zest, Auvergne saucisson, burrata with olive oil and raspberries). Proprietor Camille Fourmont oversees everything in the tiny kitchen. Not to be confused with Buvette located in the 9th arrondissement. **67 Rue Saint-Maur 75011**

Canal Saint-Martin 10TH & 19TH ARRONDISSEMENTS

RUE DE CRIMÉE

RUE CURIEL

RUE ARCHEREAU

Ⓜ 7

15

RUE RIQUET

RUE RIQUET

Ⓜ 12

Ⓜ 7

RUE MARX DORMOY

AVENUE DE FLANDRE

QUAI DE LA SEINE

14

QUAI DE LOIRE

12

13

BOULEVARD DE LA CHAPELLE

Ⓜ 2

CHÂTEAU LANDON

Ⓜ 2 5 7

JAURÈS

Ⓜ 5

RUE DE MEAUX

AVENUE

RUE ARMAND CARRE

BOULEVARD DE MAGENTA

Ⓜ 4 5 7

BOULEVARD

UX

Ⓜ 7 M

RUE M

11

RUE LA FAYETTE

RUE MATHURIN MOREAU

10

QUAI DE JEMMAPES

RUE LA FAYETTE

AVENUE CLAUDE VELLEFAUX

Ⓜ 2

BOULEVARD DE LA VILLETTE

AVENUE SIMON BOLIVAR

BOULEVARD DE MAGENTA

philippe le libraire

RUE DE LA GRANGE AUX BELLES

9

RUE SAINT-MAUR

RUE M

5

7

8

Ⓜ 2 11

6

4

Ⓜ 5

QUAI DE JEMMAPES

RUE DU FAUBOURG DU TEMPLE

BOULEVARD

3

QUAI DE VALMY

2

BOULEVARD SAINT-MAR

1

AVENUE PARMENTIER

RUE SAINT-MAUR

Ⓜ 8 5

8 9 11

RUE JEAN-PIERRE TIMBAUD

Starting point:
PLACE DE LA
RÉPUBLIQUE

What was once a working class and somewhat shady neighborhood has been wholly transformed in the last decade. It's now an aggregation of booming young businesses, and a prime picnic and drinking spot. Flanking the edge of the canal is an unmissable Parisian experience in good weather: here the public convenes in a communal urban rite, convivial and tipsily sun-kissed. The diagonal cut of the Canal St.-Martin links to the Canal de l'Ourcq by the Bassin de la Villette (the largest artificial lake in Paris), and is punctuated by arched bridges with placid views. The waterway is hugged by groups of friends, lone travelers, the occasional fisherman, and, further up, engaged games of pétanque. Boats pass leisurely through the waters; ducks (and littered beer cans) bob about.

Snaking towards Pantin, the suburb just outside of Paris, this quarter is experiencing a slow gentrification (or "embourgeoisement"). There's still a clear divide in population and lifestyle once one crosses from the 10th to the 19th arrondissement at Métro Jaurès. It is worth exploring both ends of the canal to see the city's evolution in plain sight, with some especially surprising architectural choices for subsidized housing to the north. The shifting population is not the only change to the area. The terrorist attacks on November 13, 2015 hit several cafés in the 10th arrondissement—a devastation to the city—but the spirit of the area has been unwavering in the aftermath. This thriving quarter has shown no scarring, only resilience and vitality.

❶ PLACE DE LA RÉPUBLIQUE

The Place is a central meeting point between the 3rd, 10th, and 11th arrondissements. In 1867, sculptor Gabriel Davioud designed its central fountain, decorated with lions. A bronze Marianne, the personification of the French Republic, is surrounded by three stat-

ues personifying the national motto, *liberté, égalité, fraternité*. Renovated in 2013 to make the Place a pedestrian-friendly zone, the overhauled area has been appropriated by skate boarders. After the terrorist attacks in 2015, crowds came together here to mourn and to express solidarity, and it remains a visible gathering place for both political protests and events organized by the city. Underfoot lies a busy, multi-line métro station.

❷ LA TRÉSORERIE

Showcasing tasteful housewares, this loft-like and luminous boutique has a policy of working with artisans who track their line of production very closely; sustainability and artisanal savoir-faire are privileged. The wares span enameled-steel casseroles in pastel hues, prettily patterned notebooks from Lisbon stationers, Danish-designed table linens, Savon de Marseille hand soaps by Marius Fabre, and glazed earthenware espresso cups. The venue also has a small eatery, Café Smörgås, which serves Scandinavian-style breakfast and lunch, as well as pâtisseries and coffee.
11 Rue du Château d'Eau 75010

❸ DU PAIN ET DES IDÉES

Foreigners tend to think all French bakeries are good, but there *is* a hierarchy—and this spot is at the tip-top. You can smell the *bou-*

langerie before you see it: an intoxicating buttery scent lures gourmands like an olfactory siren song. The vintage golden lettering of the signage, paired with the windows of vintage cookie tins, heralds a throwback to an old-school approach to baking. The simple pleasure of a crispy-crusted loaf of bread is made in a traditional manner, without shortcuts. It takes seven hours to make a loaf here, whereas the majority of Parisian bakers take only an hour and a half. In addition to the signature *pain des amis,* there are mini *pavés* (fist-sized, stone-oven–baked breads stuffed with spinach and goat cheese, or dried apricots with blue cheese, or bacon and figs). On the sweet side, there are puff pastry *escargots,* tarts made with fresh apples *(chaussons aux pommes),* and a butter brioche made with orange blossoms called a *mouna,* made using a North African recipe. Taste anything and everything; there are no misfires. **34 Rue Yves Toudic 75010**

4
ARTAZART

This art and design bookstore, with its bright red facade and regularly changing vitrines full of projects from ceramicists and illustrators, both reflects and draws in the creatives that hum around the canal. At the entrance is a glass case filled with Polaroid cameras; a room to the right showcases independent fashion magazines and cookbooks. There's an extensive offering of photography, art, and design books, including those linked to current exhibitions happening throughout the city. There's a room in the back dedicated to children's books (be sure to browse the cheery and visually stunning French publications by Hélium Editions and Editions MeMo). Near the cash register are notebooks and paper goods; pick up a card to send home from the local Letterpress de Paris. *83 Quai de Valmy 75010*

⑤

PHILIPPE LE LIBRAIRE

The boutique's mishmash vibe is the very best kind of chaos: a place unruly with imagination. It's hard to discern a logic, but the owner (the namesake Philippe, who opened the shop in 2007) knows where everything is. There are comics, graphic novels, zines, and illustrated wonders, as well as a selection of children's books and literature. *32 Rue des Vinaigriers 75010*

⑥ LES DOUCHES LA GALERIE

Les Douches functioned as a public bathhouse until the 1970s. Peering into the rounded doorway of the Art Deco exterior, it may not look like anything new lives on in the space, but one floor up is a superb gallery helmed by Françoise Morin since 2006. Featuring both contemporary and vintage photography, often with a focus on formal experimentalism, the space has hosted exhibitions of photography greats like Vivian Maier, Berenice Abbott, Arlene Gottfried, Ernest Haas, Ray K. Metzker, and Sabine Weiss. **5 Rue Legouvé 75010**

❼ LE VERRE VOLÉ

With its purple exterior and frosted windows, this *cave à manger* helmed by Cyril Bordarier is also a to-go bottle shop. It started as a tiny venue with a toaster in 2000; after a significant remodel in 2010, it has expanded the kitchen and dining area, yielding sophisticated results. The market menu rotates daily, while also offering staple French classics (like boudin noir with mashed potatoes). The wine selection is renowned—the front room's two walls are lined with bottles of natural stuff (it's not a full sampler; they have more in the cellars below). Worth noting: Le Verre Volé has a dedicated wine shop in the 11th arrondissement, and a small seafood-themed annex down the street. **67 Rue de Lancry 75010**

❽ LE COMPTOIR GÉNÉRALE

Behind a green gate, follow the leaf-lined path to the neon pink arrow, then push back velvet curtains into this colonial-inflected cabinet of curiosities. The two vast rooms—linked by a chandelier-overhung hallway—have glass-capped ceilings, checkered floors, raw wooden beams, and shabby-chic mismatched couches; plants and vines dangle from everywhere. In corners, curiosities like skeletons, feathers, taxidermied animals, African sorcery objects, and bones are exhibited. The huge main bar looks like the bow of a marooned pirate ship, with a scaly mermaid sculpture surveying the drinkers seeking rum-based cocktails. Over the weekend, the queues are long; pop by during the week or during the day to avoid the crowds. **80 Quai de Jemmapes 75010**

❾ TEN BELLES

Just steps from the Canal Saint-Martin, order an espresso or filter coffee with baked goods prepared in-house in the café's sprawling sister facilities in the 11th arrondissement: scones, sausage rolls, sweet buns, banana bread, brownies, and sandwiches. Grab the coveted windowed spot on the Rue de la Grange aux Belles, next to the neighboring florist. **10 Rue de la Grange aux Belles 75010**

❿ EL NOPAL

Everything is made to order at this micro taqueria (purple-painted and barely wider than a doorway). The sign features a cactus—

nopal in Spanish—and this ingredient is included in the tacos, tortas, *burróns,* and quesadillas on offer. There are no seats, so plan to eat alongside the canal. Not only is it copious, super-fresh, and accessible, it's an easy antidote to the formality of sitting in restaurants and dealing with languorous French service. ***3 Rue Eugène Varlin 75010***

⓫ POINT ÉPHÉMÈRE *(Point FMR)*

This dynamic bar and concert hall, open since 2004, is led by a team that has been turning abandoned buildings into artistic spaces for decades (including Mains d'Oeuvres in Saint-Ouen just outside of Paris). The graffiti-covered exterior is constantly transforming; in the summer, the open *terrasse* on the cobbled edge of the canal makes it perfect for lingering, that is until a fire truck whirs by (the venue's neighbor is a *caserne de pompiers,* or firehouse.) It's one of the best and cheapest places to see a concert by cool, emerging international bands. ***200 Quai de Valmy 75010***

⑫ MARIN D'EAU DOUCE

The Marin d'Eau Douce is a means of floating through the Bassin de la Villette, the Canal Saint-Martin, the Canal de l'Ourcq, and the Canal Saint-Denis. Available to rent by the hour or by the day, the self-driven, electrically-propelled boats made in the city of Nantes do not require a license and can accommodate groups of up to five, seven, or eleven people. The boats have a space at the front for picnicking and drinking (tables can be provided for an additional charge), plus they offer cushions and an awning for optimum cruising comfort. *37 Quai de la Seine 75019*

⑬ BAR OURQ

Spot the seafoam exterior: this venue along the Canal de l'Ourcq is a popular one, thanks to its unbeatable prices and well-placed corner terrace. There is mint tea, cheap beer, and strong cocktails—to be consumed in plastic goblets if you're leaving the premises—and snacky, budget-friendly finger food. Inside, it's cozy and shabby with rickety tables and couches; books, board games, and Wi-Fi are on offer. DJ sessions start in the late afternoon, starting off chill and getting wilder into the night. You can borrow a deck chair or grab pétanque balls to start a canal-side game (although the search for space itself is competitive). **68 Quai de la Loire 75019**

⑭ PANAME BREWING COMPANY

Located on the banks of the Bassin de la Villette in a building that was once a granary, Paname Brewing Company is a craft beer hub open seven days a week. Pints of artisanal beer can be enjoyed on the floating pontoon or the veranda, with a picturesque view of the water, or taken to-go if you're picnicking further down the canal. The food is easy to skip, but the in-house beers on tap—a dry IPA, a fruity lager, a licorice-y dark ale—are great, and so are the seasonally brewed specials. There's even a gluten-free beer. **41 bis Quai de la Loire 75019**

⑮ ORGUES DE FLANDRE

Translated as the "Organs of Flanders," this group of peculiar residential buildings was built between 1974 and 1980 by the architect Martin van Trek. The housing project consists of four dominating towers, which range from 25–38 floors. If uneasy venturing off the beaten path to see these extraordinarily bizarre silhouettes (which would undoubtedly give Haussmann a seizure were he alive), do check out the photographs of these and other such buildings by

young French photographer Laurent Kronental, who catalogued staggering constructions of this ilk on the fringes and outskirts of Paris. *67–107 Ave. de Flandre and 14–24 Rue Archereau 75019*

⑯ PARC DE LA VILLETTE

The Parc de la Villette is the third-largest park in Paris, located at the northeastern edge of the city. Flat and spare, it was designed by Swiss-born architect Bernard Tschumi and built between 1984 and 1987 as part of an urban redevelopment project. (The site was formerly occupied by *abattoirs*—slaughterhouses—and a wholesale meat market. Tschumi sourced his inspiration from deconstructionist philosopher Jacques Derrida, which explains the park's nontraditional design characterized by footbridges and "follies" (buildings constructed primarily for decoration)—and not much else. The park doubles as the premises for the Cité des Sciences et de l'Industrie, the largest science museum in Europe, and La Géode, an IMAX theater inside a geodesic dome. Music venues abound here, from the Philharmonie de Paris and adjacent Cité de la Musique, as well as the cast-iron-and-glass Grande Halle de la Villette. Additional concert venues include Le Cabaret Sauvage and Le Trabendo. Be sure to visit the monumental sculpture *La Bicyclette Ensevelie* (1990) by Claes Oldenburg and Coosje Van Bruggen, a seemingly sunken oversized bicycle wheel, saddle, and handlebar that partially emerge from the grasses. Festivals are common in the park and an annual open-air film festival is a Parisian summer staple. ***211 Avenue Jean Jaurès 75019***

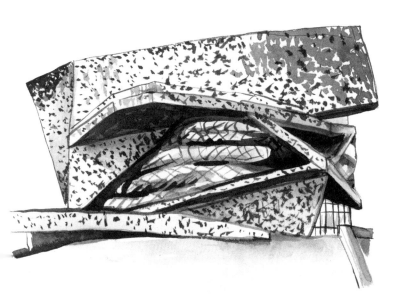

⑰ PHILHARMONIE DE PARIS

Opened in January 2015, the Jean Nouvel-designed symphonic hall shimmers from a distance. Annexing the Cité de la Musique music museum and media library, the Philharmonie has 2,400 seats distributed on all sides of the main stage and has been designed to maximize the space's ergonomic and acoustic qualities. The modular configuration allows the space to be adapted for different musical genres, ensuring optimal listening conditions. The venue is the permanent residency of the Orchestre de Paris and regularly hosts renowned national and international orchestras. The rooftop is open to the public, providing an expansive view of the city as it melds into the suburbs. *221 Avenue Jean Jaurès 75019*

HOW TO *Boulangerie*

A SHORT HISTORY OF THE BAGUETTE

The slim, crisp-crusted baguette is the icon of French culture (perhaps only rivaled by the beret) is actually defined by French law: it must weigh in at 250 grams (8.75 ounces). Derived from the Italian *bacchetta*, it means "wand" or "baton." Such loaves have been made since the time of King Louis XIV, using a steam oven brought to Paris in the early 19th century by the Austrian baker August Zang (who also introduced the croissant). The steam allows the crust to expand before setting, thus creating an airier loaf.

BAGUETTE BASICS

1. The addition of whole-wheat flour yields a *baguette de tradition française*, or simply *une tradition.*

2. Part of the traditional breakfast in France, baguettes sliced lengthwise are spread with butter and jam, known as *tartines.*

3. Sandwich-sized loaves are sometimes known as *demi-baguettes.*

A SHORT HISTORY OF THE CROISSANT

A croissant is a flaky pastry named for its crescent shape, and is made of a yeast-leavened dough layered with butter. The *kipferl*, the croissant's Austrian ancestor, has been documented as far back as the 13th century. During the baking process, the dough expands as water converts to steam, increasing the pressure between each dough layer and yielding its characteristic texture. Croissants should be consumed very soon after baking (not that anyone needs much urging).

PATISSERIE A Short Taxonomy of Traditional Sweets

Mille-feuille (translation: "cake of a thousand sheets") is traditionally made up of three layers of puff pastry *(pâte feuilletée)*, alternating with layers of pastry cream *(crème pâtissière)*. The top pastry layer is glazed with combed stripes of icing.

Mont-Blanc is a dessert of puréed sweetened chestnuts topped with whipped cream *(crème de Chantilly)*. The name stems from the mountain range it is said to resemble.

Paris–Brest is made of choux pastry and praline-flavored cream, fashioned like a wheel. Created in 1910 by Louis Durand, it commemorated the Paris–Brest–Paris bicycle race he initiated in 1891.

Religieuse, meaning "nun," is intended to represent the papal headdress. Each of two choux are filled with *crème pâtissière* (commonly chocolate or coffee) and covered in a ganache of the same flavor, then joined with piped buttercream frosting.

Tarte au citron, the prototypical lemon meringue pie, is made with shortcrust pastry, lemon custard filling, and a fluffy meringue topping.

5 PARISIAN PASTRY ADDRESSES:

Patisserie Pain de Sucre 14 Rue de Rambuteau 75004

Pâtisserie Yann Couvreur 137 Avenue Parmentier 75010

Sébastien Gaudard 22 Rue des Martyrs 75009

Des Gâteaux et du Pain 89 Rue du Bac 75007

Acide Macaron 10 Rue du Bac 75007

Rue de Charonne & Place d'Aligre, 75011

The 11th arrondissement has emerged as one of the fastest-trending regions of Paris for restaurants and nightlife. Square Aligre boasts a colorful nearly daily market surrounded by boisterous food shops, while Rue de Charonne boasts one of the best eateries in the country as well as various boutiques and cafés with terraces.

SEPTIME   Bertrand Grébaut and Théo Pourrait's bright, fresh, seasonal cooking—and a fine list of natural wines to match—is hosted within a wonderfully luminous and tasteful setting. The staff are as savvy as they are friendly. The lunch menu is a great deal; in the evening, the series of amuse-bouches and six courses are unforgettable. Booking three weeks ahead of time is basically required. **80 Rue de Charonne 75011**

CLAMATO   Again from Bertrand Grébaut, but with a more casual and seafood- and shellfish-centric menu. This venue slings out marinated fish, platters of oysters in season, razor clams with herb butter, and other elegant dispatches from the sea. Wines are natural and well-selected, just like at Septime. Take note: there are no reservations here and it's continuous service on the weekends. **80 Rue de Charonne 75011**

SEPTIME CAVE   Septime converted a sliver of a shoe-repair shop into an intimate wine bar just around the corner from their renowned restaurants. Open seven evenings a week, the *cave à vin* and bottle shop attracts locals and tourists alike—some sipping while waiting for tables at Clamato. To accompany the wine, there's a short menu of exquisite small plates (mainly cheeses and cured meats). **3 Rue Basfroi 75011**

GALERIE PATRICK SEGUIN Founded in 1989, Galerie Patrick Seguin occupies a stunning, skylit space with interiors renovated by Jean Nouvel. The venue showcases furnishings and artwork by iconic designers such as Jean Prouvé, Charlotte Perriand, Pierre Jeanneret, and Le Corbusier. **5 Rue des Taillandiers 75011**

PROMENADE PLANTÉE (COULÉE VERTE) This green beltway is the repurposed Vincennes railway line (it ceased operation in December 1969). Beginning after the Opéra Bastille, it extends eastward, intersecting the Jardin de Reuilly then becoming a grassy mall. Inaugurated in 1993, it was the only elevated park in the world until the High Line on Manhattan's West Side completed its first phase in 2009. **1 Coulée Verte René-Dumont 75012**

DERSOU The venue's brut design of concrete and cinder blocks belie its great warmth. Chef Taku Sekine's inventive, delicious plates pair with cocktails from barman Amaury Guyot. Get there for brunch on Sunday by noon for a more wallet-friendly taste. **21 Rue St.-Nicolas 75012**

BLÉ SUCRÉ Fabrice Le Bourdat, the former pastry chef at Le Bristol, makes beautiful *viennoiseries*, breads, and desserts: *kouign-amanns*, palmiers, croissants, and iced madeleines… they're best enjoyed in the leafy Square Trousseau across the street. **7 Rue Antoine Vollon 75011**

Saint-Germain-des-Prés

6TH & 14TH ARRONDISSEMENTS

134 Saint-Germain-des-Prés

1 PALAIS DES BEAUX-ARTS
   & ECOLE NATIONALE SUPÉRIEURE
   DES BEAUX-ARTS (ENSBA)

2 OFFICINE UNIVERSELLE BULY 1803

3 PORTIQUE DE SÈVRES

4 L'AVANT COMPTOIR DU MARCHÉ

5 PIERRE HERMÉ

6 ÉGLISE SAINT-SULPICE

7 JARDIN DU LUXEMBOURG

7a FONTAINE MEDICIS

7b GRAND BASSIN

7c THÉÂTRE DES MARIONETTES

8 MUSÉE ZADKINE

9 INSTITUT D'ART ET D'ARCHEOLOGIE
   & CENTRE MICHELET

10 CIMITIÈRE MONTPARNASSE

11 FONDATION HENRI CARTIER-
    BRESSON

Starting point:
PALAIS DES BEAUX-ARTS

Parisian intellectual life thrived during the après-guerre period in Saint-Germain-des-Prés, a neighborhood teeming with cafés, jazz cellars, bookstores, and publishing houses. Existentialism co-existed with blues and poetry; the neighborhood drew philosophers and artists, with an iconic cast of characters (think: Jean-Paul Sartre, Simone de Beauvoir, Jean-Luc Godard, François Truffaut) that resonates in the cultural zeitgeist even today. Le Café de Flore—as well as Le Select, La Coupole, and La Rotonde to the south, in the 14th—used to be the ultimate see-and-be-seen headquarters. Artists such as Modigliani, Soutine, Chagall, Léger, and Picasso left Montmartre for the Left Bank, where they found cheaper studios and lively nightlife.

Today, however, you'll hear anything except French philosophizing in these venues. While a locus of academia, the quarter's culti-vated vibe has has been largely supplanted by bourgeois families, tourism, and American-in-Paris aspirants channeling Hemingway. The Parisian art school is today surrounded by posh gallery spaces; experimental upstarts have long left the neighborhood. The terraces of boulevard cafés may still double as street theater, where cus-tomers are waited upon by garçons in uniform, but you're less likely to run into the next-generation Sartre and more likely to rack up a hefty bill simply for ordering coffee and an omelet. Nonetheless, a lot of history and style remain here, and the local residents, known as Germanopratins, wear this legacy very proudly.

❶ PALAIS DES BEAUX-ARTS & ECOLE NATIONALE SUPÉRIEURE DES BEAUX-ARTS (ENSBA)

Founded in 1648 by painter and art theorist Charles Le Brun, these academic buildings date as far back as the 17th century. In the 19th

century, architect François Debret and Félix Duban conceived the central Palais des Études building, embellished with majestic frescoes; Duban also commissioned historical painter Paul Delaroche to produce a colossal mural representing 75 great artists. Throughout its history, world-renowned creatives have either taught at this institution (from Marina Abramović to Gustave Moreau) or studied here (painters Jacques-Louis David, Edgar Degas, Eugène Delacroix, Claude Monet, Pierre-Auguste Renoir, as well as fashion designers Valentino Garavani and Hubert de Givenchy). The museum features end-of-year work by students, as well as temporary exhibitions. *13 Quai Malaquais and 14 Rue Bonaparte 75006*

❷ OFFICINE UNIVERSELLE BULY 1803

In 1803, Jean-Vincent Bully established a name for himself as a dis-
tiller, perfumer, and cosmetician
on Rue Saint-Honoré. The spirit of
this storied French beauty dispen-
sary was revived in the 21st century,
helmed by the same team behind
Maison Cire Trudon. Unifying contemporary cosmetics with old-
school potions, Buly offers scented
candles, incense, skin care, oils,
powders, clays, and perfumes, all in
gorgeous vintage-looking packaging.

The elegant boutique has the feel of an art-directed medicine chest
and apothecary, with carved wood cases, rows of oversized bell jars,
geometric floor tiling, and a marble sink. *6 Rue Bonaparte 75006*

❸ PORTIQUE DE SÈVRES

Just behind the church of Saint-Germain-des-Prés is a monumental ceramic portico in an Art Nouveau motif, which dates from the
Exposition Universelle of 1900. It was once the facade of an entirely
ceramic-made structure created to showcase the Manufacture
Nationale de Sèvres (one of Europe's principal porcelain manufac-
turers). Ornate yet discreetly tucked away, the structure is nestled
in the eastern corner of the Square Félix-Desruelles and features
pretty blue tones, horizontal striping, an elaborate arch, and a central
medallion. *168 bis du Boulevard Saint-Germain 75006*

4. L'AVANT COMPTOIR DU MARCHÉ

Chef Yves Camdeborde already had two sister L'Avant Comptoir locations in the neighborhood; this corner spot is his largest—though still packed elbow to elbow!—tacked onto the complex of the Marché Saint-Germain. The excellent standing-room-only dining spot has handwritten blackboard menus and plaques hung from the ceiling that one has to wriggle one's neck around to see. The walls double as a natural wine arsenal: bottles line the place top to bottom. With not-so-subtle painted pigs hung from the ceiling (Camborde comes from a family of *charcutiers*), it is a carnivore's paradise, providing hearty yet refined fare: confit pork shoulder, terrine, tripe, pâté, ham croquettas, pork dumplings, boudin noir, boudin blanc. Pots of lard are on every table to spread on wondrous slices of corn-flecked bread. Vegetarians, don't be scared to speak up; unlike at many places, here you'll be served something that matches the quality of the carnivores' selections. **14 Rue Lobineau 75006**

5. PIERRE HERMÉ

Hailing from four generations of Alsatian bakers, Pierre Hermé began his career as an apprentice to the master French *pâtissier*

Gaston Lenôtre. If Hermé learned from the best, he forged his own stalwart reputation: *Vogue* dubbed him "the Picasso of Pastry," and the title is not overblown. The first Pierre Hermé boutique opened in Tokyo in 1998, followed by a boutique in Paris in 2001 featuring pastries, macarons, and chocolates. The vitrines containing his pretty tarts and cakes evoke a French version of a Wayne Thiebaud painting. Hermé succeeds magnificently at reinventing heavy-handed traditional recipes with delicacy and modernity: his pastry decor is minimalist and he has stated that he "uses sugar like salt, in other words, as a seasoning to heighten other shades of flavor."

72 Rue Bonaparte
75006

❻ ÉGLISE SAINT-SULPICE

Dedicated to Sulpitius the Pious, this Roman Catholic church is the second largest in the city (it is only slightly smaller than Notre-Dame). The present edifice, for which construction began in 1646, was erected to replace a church initially built in the 13th century. The neoclassical design features large arched windows that fill the vast interior with light. Eugène Delacroix painted murals within its walls, most famously *Jacob Wrestling with the Angel* and *Heliodorus Driven from the Temple*. The church has a long-standing tradition

of talented organists dating back to the 18th century, and Sunday organ recitals are held regularly. Fun fact: The Marquis de Sade and Charles Baudelaire were baptized here (in 1740 and 1821, respectively). The church also was where French novelist and playwright Victor Hugo got married in 1822. *2 Rue Palatine 75006*

❼ JARDIN DU LUXEMBOURG

This park has a certain relaxed feel that belies its formal landscaping: it's a park that the locals use and one very much associated with childhood, thanks to its iconic toy boat–strewn basin and rides on dutifully trotting ponies. Situated on the border between Saint-Germain-des-Prés and the Latin Quarter, the Luxembourg Gardens were inspired by the Florentine Boboli Gardens, at the initiative of Queen Marie de Medici in 1612, a complement to the Luxembourg

Palace. After the French Revolution, Jean Chalgrin, the architect of the Arc de Triomphe, tweaked the Italianate garden to have more of a French style. There are 106 statues sprinkled throughout, doubling as monuments to writers like Charles Baudelaire and Paul Verlaine. There are many draws for children such as puppet shows, a vintage carousel, and a playground, as well as diversions for adults such as chess tables and tennis courts.

The garden today is owned by the French Senate (who meet in the palace). The gardens feature in Victor Hugo's novel *Les Misérables,* Henry James's *The Ambassadors,* and the final scene of William Faulkner's *Sanctuary.* **Boulevard Saint-Michel/Rue de Vaugirard/ Bue Guynemer 75006**

⑦ₐ FONTAINE MEDICIS

The fountain (built in the early 17th century as a nympheum and artificial grotto) was designed by Tommaso Francini, a Florentine fountain maker and hydraulic engineer. The long water basin is flanked by plane trees, and sculptures by French classical sculptor Auguste Ottin were added to the grotto's rockwork. **Jardin du Luxembourg, Rue de Vaugirard 75006**

7b
GRAND BASSIN

An especially scenic and iconic spot, children may rent boats by the hour from a small kiosk and nudge the tiny skips around the pond. Green park chairs are gathered around in clusters, where people lounge in the sun. *Jardin du Luxembourg, 2 Rue Auguste Comte 75006*

7c
THÉÂTRE DES MARIONETTES

This puppet theater, the largest of its kind with a capacity for more than 250 spectators, has been in existence since 1933. It features Guignol, that central player of the *marionnettes françaises*, characterized as both silly and clever. This theater was founded by Robert Desarthis, who was the progeny of a toymaker; his son has taken over in keeping with the family legacy. *Jardin du Luxembourg 75006*

❽ MUSÉE ZADKINE

This studio-turned-museum—along with that of sculptor Antoine Bourdelle, located nearby behind the Montparnasse train station—provides a peek into the local artists' scene of the 20th century. Ossip Zadkine (1890–1967) was a sculptor of Russian origin who lived and worked on these premises between 1928 and 1967. It's a quick visit, but a charming one. The petite garden is peppered with wood, stone, and clay sculptures, spotlighting both Zadkine's human silhouettes and abstract arabesques. ***100 bis Rue d'Assas 75006***

❾ INSTITUT D'ART ET D'ARCHEOLOGIE & CENTRE MICHELET

Amid all the Haussmannian beige, this building literally hits like a ton of bricks. The art history departments for the universities Paris I and Paris IV are headquartered here; it also held a once-important reference library whose contents have since migrated. The building was designed between 1925 and 1930 by architect Paul Bigot, who studied (and then became a professor) at the École des Beaux-Arts. Since 1996, it has been classified a historical monument. **6 Avenue de l'Observatoire and 3 Rue Michelet 75006**

❿ CIMITIÈRE MONTPARNASSE

Created in 1824, this burial site has many famed figures from France's intellectual and artistic elite—as well as ex-pats who made Paris their home. The list of minds laid to rest would make for the best dinner party: Brassaï (1899–1984), photographer; Constantin Brâncuși (1876–1957), sculptor; Charles Baudelaire (1821–67), poet; Marguerite Duras (1914–96), author; Serge Gainsbourg (1928–91), singer; Chris Marker (1921–2012), filmmaker; Frédéric Bartholdi (1834–1904), sculptor of the Statue of Liberty; Man Ray (1890–1976), photographer; Eric Rohmer (1920–2010), film director; Samuel Beckett (1906–89), playwright; Jean Seberg (1938–79), actress; Susan Sontag (1933–2004), author. The

French philosopher Jean-Paul Sartre (1905–80) and feminist author Simone de Beauvoir (1908–86) are, despite their tumultuous love story, buried in the same grave. In the realm of iconic political figures, there is the grave of Alfred Dreyfus (1859–1935), the Jewish military officer falsely accused of treason during the Dreyfus Affair, and more recently Georges Wolinski (1934–2015), the political cartoonist assassinated in the Paris offices of the publication *Charlie Hebdo* on January 7, 2015. **3 Boulevard Edgar Quinet 75014**

⓫ FONDATION HENRI CARTIER-BRESSON

This gem showcases the *crème de la crème* of photography history. The venue was established in 2003 by Henri Cartier-Bresson, his wife Martine Franck (a photographer in her own right), and their daughter. The venue preserves the two photographers' archives (vintage prints, contact sheets, drawings, publications, rare books, correspondence), while temporary exhibitions celebrate other photographers, from Francesca Woodman to Pieter Hugo to Saul Leiter.

There are regularly organized conversations about photography practices and the milieu from experts, and there's an on-site library accessible to researchers. The foundation is currently housed in a building designed by architect Emile Molinié in 1912, but has acquired a larger and more central space in the Marais at 79 Rue des Archives. The institution is expected to transfer to this venue in autumn 2018. *2 Impasse Lebouis, 75014*

Champs de Mars 75007

The 7th arrondissement includes that near-mandatory double tourist attraction: the Eiffel Tower and the Champ de Mars (named after the Roman god of war, since the lawns were formerly used by the French military). The affluent residential arrondissement contains a number of national institutions, foreign diplomatic embassies, and hôtels particuliers (mansions).

EIFFEL TOWER The three-level wrought-iron latticed monument—named after engineer Gustave Eiffel, whose company designed and built the tower—was constructed for the entrance to the 1889 *Exposition Universelle*. Virulently criticized initially, it has become a global cultural icon practically a synecdoche for France itself! ***Champ de Mars, 5 Avenue Anatole France 75007***

LAVIROTTE BUILDING Jules Aimé Lavirotte (1864–1929) was a French architect best known for his ornamental Art Nouveau exteriors (replete with ceramic tiles, wrought-iron balconies, and floral sculptures). This building, dating from 1901, is his most flamboyant work, a vision of lavish craftsmanship. Lavirotte also designed nearby buildings at 12 Rue Sedillot and 3 Square Rapp; the latter was his own residence. ***29 Avenue Rapp 75007***

ÉCOLE MILITAIRE This complex, opened in 1760, houses various military-training facilities. Napoleon Bonaparte attended in 1784, graduating in one year instead of two. ***1 Place Joffre 75007***

PONT DE GRENELLE This bridge, which crosses over a small artificial island within the Seine (the Île aux Cygnes), has a quarter-scale replica of the Statue of Liberty. Installed nearly three years after its U.S. counterpart in July 1889, it faces west, in the direction of its sibling in New York City. **Pont de Grenelle 75007**

MAISON DE LA CHANTILLY Specializing in whipped cream (a.k.a. *"crème Chantilly"* in French, first whisked up for Louis XIV in the Château de Chantilly's kitchen), this shop is a dream spot for any sweet tooth. Did you know that Chantilly alone is deemed a perfectly suitable dessert in France? **47 Rue Cler 75007**

O COFFEESHOP Helmed by an Australian and French duo, the café attracts a local clientele. Grab a slice of homemade toasty-warm banana bread with a cup of specialty coffee. **23 Rue de Lourmel 75015**

MUSÉE DU QUAI BRANLY Opened in 2006, this museum showcases indigenous art from Africa, Asia, Oceania, and the Americas. The proposal for such a museum was spearheaded in 1990 by the ethnologist and art collector Jacques Kerchache 'in a manifesto published in the newspaper *Libération*. The collection spans 450,000 objects, 3,500 of which are on display at any given time. The building was designed by French architect Jean Nouvel. **37 Quai Branly 75007**

MUSÉE RODIN Opened in 1919, the museum's collection includes Auguste Rodin's most iconic creations—including *The Thinker*, *The Kiss*, and *The Gates of Hell*. The 18th-century mansion (and lovely garden) is housed in Hôtel Biron; which formerly hosted such tenants as Jean Cocteau, Henri Matisse, and Isadora Duncan before the sculptor appropriated the place as his studio. The closest Métro stop, Varenne, features Rodin sculptures on the platform. **79 Rue de Varenne 75007**

Museum Hub 75016

The 16th arrondissement—one of the most prestigious and wealthy sectors of the city, with views of the Seine and the Eiffel Tower—features a concentration of museums between the Place du Trocadéro and the Place d'Iéna.

PALAIS DE TOKYO is the

largest contemporary art museum in France. Housed in a monumental building, constructed in 1937 for the international exhibition *Arts and Techniques in Modern Life*, it was completely renovated in 2011–2012. The brut, labyrinthine venue showcases ambitious exhibitions and elaborate live performances in an area of more than 72,000 square feet (22,000 m²) spread over four floors—plus two restaurants and a bookshop. With no permanent collection, it produces all of its exhibitions, which have ranged from a carte blanche accorded to performance artist Tino Sehgal to installations by author Michel Houellebecq. Its exceptionally late hours are worth exploiting. It is open till midnight. **13 Avenue du Président-Wilson 75116**

MUSÉE D'ART MODERNE DE LA VILLE DE PARIS,

also constructed for the *International Exhibition of Arts and Technology* like its neighbor, is dedicated to modern and contemporary art of the 20th and 21st centuries. Amongst the 10,000 items in the collection are works by Robert and Sonia Delaunay, Giorgio de

Chirico, Alexander Calder, Alberto Giacometti, Jean Dubuffet, Yves Klein, Bridget Riley, Robert Rauschenberg, amongst others. *11 Avenue du Président-Wilson 75116*

PALAIS GALLIERA was constructed in 1879, based upon

a palace owned by the Duchess Galliera in Genoa. The opulent Italian Renaissance-style edifice was executed by architect Léon Ginain, with a steel underframe constructed by the Eiffel Company. Since 1977, it has been a fashion museum with rotating exhibitions of garments and accessories from the 18th century to the present day. (It will inaugurate a permanent display of its vast collections in 2018). The museum's holdings contain about 70,000 items: including gloves owned by Sarah Bernhardt; outfits worn by Marie-Antoinette; and garments from leading 19th- and 20th- century designers including Christian Dior, Jean Paul Gaultier, Givenchy, Yves Saint Laurent, and Elsa Schiaparelli. The Palais Galliera faces Square Brignole-Galliera, a pretty and serene spot to catch one's breath. *Rue de Galliera, 10 Avenue Pierre 1er de Serbie 75116*

MUSÉE GUIMET, founded by industrialist Emile Guimet, encompasses a large collection of Asian art. The museum opened in Lyon in 1879 but was later transferred to Paris, re-opening in 1889 in a neoclassical building by architect Jules Chatron. Devoted to far-flung travel, Guimet was commissioned by a public minister to study the religions of the Far East, and the museum contains the fruits of this expedition, including a collection of Chinese and Japanese porcelain. There is also art from Afghanistan, the Himalayas, Korea, and India. *6 Place d'Iéna 75116*

Starting point:
MÉTRO
LAMARCK-
CAULAINCOURT

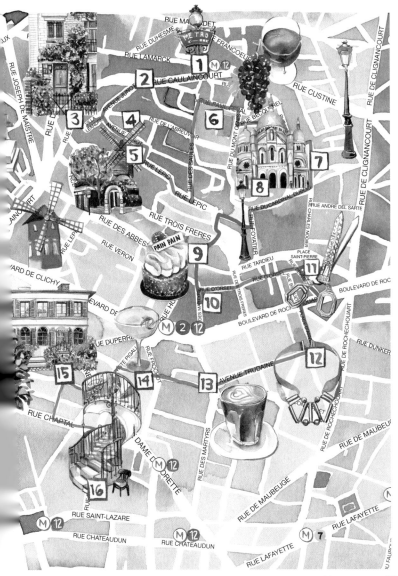

Butte Montmartre was once a village with orchards, far offset from the center of Paris, in a "countryside" context that provided a view of Paris below. (Later it was a hotbed for louche cabaret fun.) The area retains a village quality, and is slightly removed from the rest of town in its northern heights. At the very top, cobbled residential streets give way to tourist zeal (avoid Place du Tertre at all costs). At the very bottom, Boulevard de Clichy is lined with kebab joints and sex shops, though the area has become more and more gentrified. In between: beautiful residences and former artist workshops interspersed with traces of history—windmills, a hillside parcel with vines, the Sacré-Coeur basilica and its breathtaking view. It's easy to curse the endless vertical stairways, but there are many draws to motivate a climb up the hills.

❶ MÉTRO LAMARCK–CAULAINCOURT

The station, which opened in 1912 as part the city's northward extension, takes its name from the two roads that cross at its

entrance: the Chevalier de Lamarck, after a 19th-century French naturalist (whose legacy is his theory on the inheritance of acquired traits), and the marquis de Caulaincourt, named for a 19th century general, ambassador, and foreign minister.

② AVENUE JUNOT

Avenue Junot, a beautiful and quiet curved stretch, was created at the turn of the 20th century, when the neighborhood was rife with rag-and-bone men and *bohèmes*. The rows of residences include some notable architectural gems. Number 1, behind the Moulin de la Galette, used to be a theater; it was refurbished in 1983 by director Claude Lelouch for a film. Number 15 was built by Czech-born architect and theorist Adolf Loos; avant-garde poet/performance artist Tristan Tzara, one of the founders of the Dada movement, resided there. Number 39 was once a hotel where Edith Piaf had a room and received visits from her then-lover, the singer Yves Montand. **Avenue Junot 75018**

③ VILLA LÉANDRE

A visit to Villa Léandre, a bucolic cul-de-sac, feels like wandering into a tiny hamlet. The Anglo-Saxon-style brick buildings and brightly colored shutters, in blue and turquoise, are overrun with flowers in the spring. Built in the 1920s, it was named after Charles Léandre, a painter and caricaturist who was a Montmartre local. **Villa Léandre 75018**

❹ SQUARE SUZANNE BUISSON

Square Suzanne Buisson bears the name of the militant Socialist and feminist who was deported by the Gestapo. You'd never know the weight of history from the tranquil environs, however: the tiered structure has an entrance featuring an Art Deco-style burrstone-made rotunda, and games of *boules* are often

played by the older generations among the plane and poplar trees.
7 bis Rue Girardon 75018

❺ MOULIN DE LA GALETTE

This windmill, built in 1622, is so startling and anachronistic it feels plucked from a movie set. The mill's 19th-century owners, the Debray family, not only made popular *galettes* using mill-ground flour, but also oversaw a bumping dance hall and cabaret, where the working classes, the bohemian creatives, and the "slumming" bourgeois indulged in a glass of local Montmartre wine with bread. Many artists immortalized Le Moulin de la Galette: Pierre-Auguste Renoir's interpretation was sun-dappled and festive (*Bal du Mou-*

lin de la Galette, 1876) while Henri de Toulouse-Lautrec depicted a murkier, leerier scene (*Au Bal du Moulin de la Galette*, 1889). **83 Rue Lepic 75018**

❻ VIGNE DE MONTMARTRE

A relic of the wine-growing tradition in the Île-de-France, these un-expected Parisian vines (a third of an acre, or 0.15 hectare) were once a money-making means for a local abbey. They still grow at the corner of Rue des Saules and Rue St. Vincent. Threatened with

demolition in the 19th century, the parcel was protected thanks to vociferous local outcry. Today the vines are maintained year-round by the city's parks department, with the cultivation carried out in local wine cellars. The *crû* it yields is called the Clos Montmartre, and the sales (about 500 liters, or 132 gallons, produced annually) go to local nonprofit causes, although the wine is considered *piquette*, or rather mediocre. Since the 1930s, during the second weekend in October, the neighborhood celebrates the *Fête des Vendanges* with music, parades, and full wineglasses. **Rue des Saules and Rue Saint Vincent 75018**

❽ LE GRAND 8

The Angers-born proprietor's red-fronted bistro is a veritable winemaker's hub, with hearty fare, friendly service, a tiny terrace, and a panoramic view of Paris. The restaurant serves unpretentious, well-executed dishes using organic, artisanal produce, from lamb chops to rumsteak, duck breast to free-range pork. Hundreds of ever changing, lesser known natural wines will surprise and delight even the wine-savviest. You'll likely be dining among the *vignerons* themselves, as the place is such an industry draw. **8 Rue Lamarck 75018**

❽ SACRÉ-COEUR BASILICA & VIEW

A prime perch for overlooking Paris, this swarming sector of Montmartre brings out the tourists (as well as sellers of plastic trinkets and painted mimes). The view of the city from the forecourt of the basilica is irreproachably breathtaking—one can see the surrounding countryside for 30 miles (50 km), and it is the highest point in Paris after the Eiffel Tower. Try not to let the crowds dim the wonder!

The church was meant to be a spiritual balm when France was defeated and partially occupied by German troops in the late 19th century. In 1874, architect Paul Abadie won the public competition with his Romano-Byzantine design in travertine stone (although six other architects succeeded him to complete the structure). The church was inspired by such architectural marvels as Saint Sofia in Constantinople and San Marco in Venice. The first stone was laid in 1875 and the Basilica (sans dome) was inaugurated in 1891. In 1895, the almost 21-ton (19-metric-ton) bell was donated. The imposing size of the grand pipe organ, built in 1898, is one of the most remarkable in France. *35 Rue du Chevalier-de-la-Barre 75018*

❾ CHINEMACHINE

This vintage boutique *(or friperie)* stocks a mélange of high/low brands—"H&M to Hermès, Forever21 to Fendi," often buying garments from Parisians emptying their wardrobes. Shuffle carefully through the piles of jeans and leather pieces from various decades. The decor includes old mannequins, vintage photos, and a record player; there is also a sister location in the 10th arrondissement. *100 Rue des Martyrs 75018*

⑩ L'OBJET QUI PARLE

L'Objet Qui Parle—"the Object that Speaks"—brings vintage French tokens to the forefront. This tiny shop is filled with decorative oddities, and can barely fit more than a half-dozen shoppers at one time. It's a veritable cabinet of curiosities filled with glass bottles, hotel bells, family portraits, enamel tins, baroque mirrors, antlers, taxidermied skulls, vintage dishes, miniature altars and religious artifacts, glass cloches of every size, butterflies englobed in transparent medallions, Napoleon III inspired furniture, and crystal chandeliers. The owner and founder opened the store in 1988; he travels in France's northeast Alsace and Lorraine regions, scouts for treasures, and provides items for set designers, film shoots, and department stores. **86 Rue des Martyrs 75018**

⑪ FABRIC DISTRICT MARCHÉ SAINT-PIERRE

If Le Sentier is where most Paris fashion designers shop for their collections, day-to-day Parisians come to the Marché Saint-Pierre district for their self fashioning needs. The area is teeming with rolls of fabric and fixings of all colors and tastes. Be sure to stop by **Tissu Reine,** a multi floor fabric department store that carries Liberty print fabrics, silk thread, tassels, notions, household linens, and

Eiffel Tower–shaped embroidery scissors. **Coupons Dreyfus,** if less neat and polished than its neighbor, has its own charms: a wooden cash register kiosk, mannequins in froufrou sparkly dresses, and—best of all—a wonderful view of Sacré-Cœur from the 4th floor, visible when wedged between bolts of velour. *3–5 Place Saint-Pierre and 2 Rue Charles Nodier 75018*

⓬ MARION VIDAL

Designer Marion Vidal started her eponymous label in 2004; an airy and minimalist boutique followed in 2012. Vidal studied architecture in Paris and Milan before venturing into fashion in Antwerp. Today she collaborates with Italian artisans who provide beautiful raw materials, and the bijoux are then assembled in her Parisian atelier. The geometric configurations nimbly blend form and volume. She also designs for labels like Céline, Christofle, and Lacoste, and even participated in an Iris Apfel pop-up collaboration, showcased at chic department store Le Bon Marché. *13 Avenue Trudaine 75009*

⓭ KB CAFÉ SHOP

Inaugurated by a Frenchie who spent time in Australia, this spot was one of the first to bring specialty coffee to Paris when it opened in 2010. In addition to quality coffee, all treats like carrot cakes and scones are made in-house. You're

not shunned for using a laptop here, which can be either a pro or a con. Score a spot on the terrace, which is the perfect roost for tracking the bourgeois locals and ex-pats ambling up and down Rue des Martyrs. *53 Avenue Trudaine 75009*

⑭ ENTRÉE DES ARTISTES

Spread over two floors, this bar has sleek design fixtures (marble surfaces, brick walls, dim lighting, turntables spinning disco and soul) paired with excellent drinks and small plates to share. The cocktail menu spans from light and fresh to dry and spiced, and might include anything from beet juice to tobacco liqueur to wasabi syrup. Try a fizzed-up Pisco (infused with thyme, lemon, ginger, and honey syrup) or a more classic Boulevardier (Bourbon, Campari, and Vermouth rouge). There's also a natural wine list. The fare's seasonal options rotate, but samples include hearty beef cheek and risotto, cod with parsnip purée and artichokes, or squid, Treviso, and hazelnuts. *30 Rue Victor Massé 75009*

⑯ MUSÉE DE LA VIE ROMANTIQUE

Ary Scheffer, a Dutch-born painter of the Romantic school, settled on Rue Chaptal in 1830. His home doubled as a hub for intellec-

tual gatherings; he received George Sand, Franz Liszt, and Charles Dickens. Chopin plucked away at his Pleyel piano; Delacroix was his neighbor. The small property remained in private hands until it became a museum in 1982. The garden has a café, a lovely and peaceful spot—as much of a draw as the museum itself. *16 Rue Chaptal 75009*

16 MUSÉE GUSTAVE MOREAU

Artist Gustave Moreau, born in 1826, sourced inspiration from Romantic and Italianized styles, referencing canonical artists like Michelangelo and Leonardo da Vinci. Often alluding to biblical myths, he sought to address the fervor of the soul, the natural world, and the imagination—expressed in skillful detail and vivid palettes. He befriended Théodore Chassériau, a former pupil of the painter

Jean-Auguste-Dominique Ingres, as well as young Edgar Degas, whom he met in Italy while touring the country copying the masters. From 1892–98, he was a professor at the École des Beaux-Arts; Henri Matisse was a student.

In 1852, his parents bought him the house at 14 Rue de La Rochefoucauld, which was converted into a museum in 1895. The peculiar, wonderful interiors feature, among other things, a stunning spiral staircase. *14 Rue de la Rochefoucauld 75009*

HOW TO DECIPHER
Parisian Architecture

AN ABBREVIATED HISTORY OF HAUSSMANNIAN PARIS

Paris is one of the most walkable cities thanks to its ingenious urban planning, with infrastructures and superstructures that maximize urban density while also enabling fluid connectivity. The urban fabric was reconfigured at a radical scale in under two decades: a network of roads, avenues, city blocks, homogenized buildings, plus the implementation of potable water and sewage systems.

Napoleon III, the first elected president of France, started the ambitious project in 1850. Wishing to extend the Rue de Rivoli and create a new park (the Bois de Boulogne) on the outskirts of the city, he grew impatient with the slow pace of progress and searched for an exacting new prefect to help carry out his urban renewal program. In 1853, Georges-Eugène Haussmann was selected to usher forward new public works and make the city healthier, less congested, and better-looking, with more light, air, and trees.

For nearly two decades, most of Paris was an enormous construction site. One in five Parisian workers was employed in the building trade; thousands of workers were hired to improve the sanitation and circulation of the city. The reconstruction was the largest such public works project ever undertaken in Europe; never had a major city been completely rebuilt while it was still *intact*. Workers tore down old buildings (including the house in which Haussmann himself was born, symbolically enough) and cut nearly 50 miles (80 km) of new avenues to form arteries throughout the city.

To provide for those forced out from the city center during construction—and to accommodate the growing population at large—Haussmann widened the city's boundaries and annexed surrounding communes. He increased the number of arrondissements from 12 to 20—still the configuration today. Haussmann's method for financing the radical redevelopment was as follows: the government expropriated old buildings, compensated the owners, and private companies built new streets and buildings by Haussmannian standards, which they could then develop and sell.

← SERVANT QUARTERS (SLANTED ROOF) →

← CONTINUOUS BALCONY →

← IDENTICAL CEILING HEIGHT →

← HIGH CEILINGS & BALCONY →

← COMMERCIAL SPACE →

Buildings were required to be the same height, encompassing a reconfigurable street-facing ground floor intended as a commercial space; a mezzanine; a second story *piano nobile* with high ceilings and a balcony; third and fourth floors with identical ceiling heights; a fifth floor with a continuous balcony; a sixth floor with the lowest ceiling (to house the servants under slanted mansard roofs). The walls were thin and shared; the exteriors were designed along a grid, and were faced with cream-colored cut limestone extracted from quarries in the Oise. The sober aesthetic stayed within a limited stylistic vocabulary and compacted form, creating the signature harmonious look of Parisian boulevards, which did not change until the advent of Art Nouveau at the turn of the 20th century.

Napoleon III also wanted to build supplementary parks and gardens, particularly in the new neighborhoods of the expanding city. Inspired by Londonian green spaces, especially Hyde Park, he oversaw the creation of the Bois de Boulogne to the west, the Bois de Vincennes to the east, the Parc des Buttes-Chaumont to the north, and Parc Montsouris to the south. The city's older parks (Parc Monceau, Jardin du Luxembourg) were redesigned and replanted. He also created localized small-scale parks and gardens, so that no resident was more than a ten-minute walk from greenery.

The French parliament increasingly criticized Napoleon III regarding Haussmann and his spending, to the point that the prefect was forced to resign in 1870. Haussmann died in Paris in 1891, at the age of 82, and is buried in Père Lachaise Cemetery.

Haussmann's Paris inspired urban planning in capitals like Brussels, Rome, Vienna, Stockholm, Madrid, and Barcelona. His work also inspired the City Beautiful Movement in the United States: Frederick Law Olmsted, who designed Central Park in New York, was awed by the Bois de Boulogne during a trip to Europe.